1966

The
Burning
Seal

The
Burning
Seal

by

M. Brunilde Probst

Biography of
Mother Mary Clara Pfaender
Foundress of the Franciscan Sisters
of Salzkotten

FRANCISCAN HERALD PRESS
Publishers of Franciscan Literature
Chicago 9, Illinois

THE BURNING SEAL
by M. Brunilde Probst
Library of Congress Catalog Card Number: 60-11992
Published by Franciscan Herald Press,
    1434 West 51st Street, Chicago 9, Illinois
Copyright, 1960, by Franciscan Sisters, Daughters
    of the Sacred Hearts of Jesus and Mary, Wheaton, Illinois
Designed by Publication Associates

+++

Nihil Obstat
    Rt. Rev. Msgr. Romeo Blanchette O.F.M.
    Censor Librorum
Imprimatur
    †Martin D. McNamara
    Bishop of Joliet

June 10, 1960

Foreword

October 5, 1957

is the anniversary of the death of our revered Foundress, Mother M. Clara Pfaender. The grateful love which we owe her has induced us to present this, her biographical sketch, for the 2500 Sisters who call themselves her daughters in Germany, France, United States of America, the Netherlands, and Indonesia. The publication of this biography was made possible through the detailed preliminary studies of the late Monsignor John Schaefer, who was for many years the Ecclesiastical Moderator of the German Province of the congregation. That we are now able to present the portrait of our Mother—truly admirable because of her trying ordeal—we owe to his zealous research of the history of the congregation and of the authoritative archives. Reflection upon the human and supernatural aspects of this likeness bestows upon us much practical wisdom and wins for the noble personality of our Mother Foundress the esteem of all who meet her in *The Burning Seal.*

On the feast of St. Clare, 1957

> The Superiors of the Congregation
> Franciscan Sisters of Salzkotten

Contents

Preface

GOD'S WAYS ARE WONDERFUL IN ACHIEVING THE PURPOSES for which man was created, namely, the greater glory of God and the salvation of man's soul. To attain these ends, God has watched over mankind, supplying specific means for every age.

When the wildernesses of America were developing into towns, villages, and cities; when the education of its youth, the care of its sick and aged were gradually becoming serious problems for the pastors, God was raising up new communities in Europe that could supply the forthcoming help so necessarily needed and wanted in the New World. Later, when the Kulturkampf afflicted the religious in Germany, God effected the transfer of members of many communities to America.

One of these communities, the Franciscan Sisters, Daughters of the Sacred Hearts of Jesus and Mary, founded by Venerable Mother M. Clara Pfaender in Salzkotten, Germany, was requested to send nurses to conduct a hospital in Carondelet, Missouri. Mother Clara had a surplus of Sisters on hand because of the stringent laws of the Kulturkampf, and she thought also of the future welfare of the community when she consented to send several groups of Sisters to America. One of these groups, consisting of five Sisters, set sail from Bremen in December, 1875. The ship foundered and went aground on the sandbanks off the coast of England. All five Sisters heroically lost their lives in the icy waters. These are the Sisters lovingly depicted by Gerard Manley Hopkins in the "Wreck of the Deutschland."

A Provincial Motherhouse and another hospital were established in St. Louis, Missouri. From here, the Sisters traveled north, south, and west establishing hospitals, schools, orphanages, and homes for working girls. In 1947, the Provincial Motherhouse was transferred from St. Louis, Missouri, to Wheaton, Illinois.

The
Burning
Seal

1

A pilgrim before St. Peter's

AUTUMN, 1882. MORNING DAWNS ABOVE ROME, BUT THE
Holy City is still slumbering. In the east, the first rays of
dawn appear, directed as if in greeting toward the golden
cross on the lofty cupola of St. Peter's. As soon as the light
penetrates the gray mist of morning, the procession of pilgrims
begins streaming toward the Cathedral of the World—wave
upon wave—people from far and near.

Each pilgrim arrives as a newcomer. By their clothing,
countenance, and bearing, one can gain a hint of what they
seek at St. Peter's. The cross has already seen many guests
who pass by hurriedly. These are not numbered among the
faithful. Others consider themselves fortunate to be home at
last within the Eternal City. And what of those marked by
suffering? The cross also looks down on them. For these suf-
ferers it holds a special blessing in readiness.

The pilgrims of Autumn, 1882, present a constantly changing picture. Yet surely the Swiss guards of St. Peter's must
wonder about the tall woman who has appeared among the
pilgrims day after day for two years. She wears a coarse brown
habit and is girded with a white cord. She is well into her fifties.
Sorrow stamps her countenance, but her manner is calm and
her features, framed in a white linen coif with a black veil,

are composed. Evidently she is a daughter of St. Francis, but her garb is unknown in Rome. In the Eternal City there is no convent in which such religious reside.

Morning after morning this mysterious pilgrim is one of the first to stand at the door of St. Peter's. Are her eyes actually filled with tears as she approaches and greets the cross? She remains a long time in St. Peter's. As she leaves, her step does not seem lighter, but her countenance is more serene and, perhaps, more resigned. She has had nothing to eat since the day before, and she has knelt for hours at the tomb of the Apostle. However, this is only the prelude to her daily pilgrimage. Now she will wend her way from church to church until the last Angelus rings out over the Holy City.

Thus it has gone on for months.

Occasionally, she is seen in the office of the Cardinal Vicar. Her right hand, which holds a document that must be important to her, seems to tremble. Her left hand closes tightly about the large crucifix which hangs at her side. Bowed and depressed, she leaves the Vicariate and wearily makes her way back to a little room she has taken in the home of a German woman. Is it possible that she, too, is German? In the early dawn, the door of the little house opens and permits the pilgrim to step over the threshold; in the evening, it stands open to offer her hospitality for the night.

But the woman's pace is gradually slackening as she daily wends her way from church to church. Her tall figure is losing some of its vigor, and her head droops wearily. Finally, on one morning the guards of St. Peter's look in vain for the woman in the brown habit. She fails to appear. When she finally does come forth again, she is marked by sickness. Supporting herself on the arm of a nurse, she moves painfully to the nearby hospital on the Campo Santo.

Weeks pass, and then one day a quiet procession makes its way from the hospital to the Church of SS. Vincent and

Anastasius. The nurse, who recently led the pilgrim to the sanatorium, and the German woman, who offered her shelter in her home, follow a brown pine casket with a bronze cross as a sole ornament—a reflection of the golden cross on St. Peter's.

In the church's chantry, the coffin is set down and opened. The pilgrim now rests within its narrow confines. Her features are at peace, but around the motionless lips lie faint lines of pain. Do these lips still have something to impart? Or do they have a secret to guard? Death has pressed them together with its seal.

Casual worshippers come and go; they wonder for a few moments about the mysterious dead person, then forget her. The more charitable offer a prayer before they go their way. After two days the coffin is closed and, attended by several Germans, is taken to the cemetery of San Lorenzo. In the shadow of the church of St. Lawrence, the patron of the sick and poor, a grave is dug for the pilgrim from Germany.

Who was she? Only a few of those who accompanied the dead body knew her name; and that name offered them no clue. But in the register of the cemetery of San Lorenzo, the following was entered on the 7th of October, 1882:

MOTHER MARY CLARA PFAENDER
Foundress of the Congregation of the Franciscan Sisters of Salzkotten

With this notice the pilgrim's secret was not revealed. Who was Mother Clara Pfaender? To what work did she devote her life and love? As Mother, why did she not remain in the midst of her daughters? What drove her to Rome and caused her to wander as a pilgrim from sanctuary to sanctuary, knocking on the very portals of the Vatican until October 5, 1882, when, only 55 years old, she was given merciful refuge in the arms of Brother Death?

From the golden cross on St. Peter's, under whose victorious rays the pilgrim rests, back to the first little cross that a pious mother impressed on the forehead of a newborn child, is a far way—a way of the cross with countless stations. To each station adheres the bloody trace of a painful struggle between human nature and a grace-laden vocation.

2

The obedient child

WINTER REIGNED SUPREME IN GERMANY. BUT IN NO OTHER place did it reign more royally than in the mountains of southern Westphalia. Thus, at least, was it said with proud satisfaction by the people who lived in this forest region. Like a gigantic sugar cone, the Kahle Asten towered above a dark wave of pointed pines which peered out from beneath the mantle of snow. In the valley, the river Nuhne flowed swiftly between ice-crusted banks.

Hallenberg, a little city on the southeastern slope of the mountain, is a privileged child of nature. The scenery is beautiful both in summer and in winter, and one may look upwards to the proud heights of the mountains, and downwards into the charming valley of the Nuhne. Hallenberg's mayor, Henry Pfaender, and his young wife, Caroline Wahle, celebrated a double Advent during the winter of 1827—the holy coming of the Lord and the joyful arrival of their first child. The child, a healthy girl, was born on the first Thursday of Advent, December 6. The hand of the mother traced the sign of the cross on the forehead of her daughter. And how much this child would need the blessing!

As the bells of the old parish church of Hallenberg resounded across the snow-covered roofs on the following Sunday, the little girl was carried to church for baptism. Prior to the birth of the child, the mother expressed the wish that the child be re-born as soon as possible in the waters of sanctifying grace. The father, although a Protestant, showed himself agreeable, for he remembered what he had promised at the altar—that the children be baptized and reared as Catholics. Young Anna Theresa was the first of five Pfaender children. Every year a new child was baptized, and work and joy reigned in the mayor's home. But anxiety soon came to mar the happiness of the family.

The mother became ill, and the father was helpless. Who would manage the household? Who would take care of the helpless little ones? The mother's younger sister offered to substitute as well as she could.

Little Theresa, by nature a thoughtful and serious child, frequently sat for long periods at the bedside of her good mother. Did the mother have a premonition that she would soon have to leave her children? Perhaps, for she made use of the days which remained to her for the education of her oldest daughter, and with motherly concern laid a firm religious foundation into the heart of her child. Her little girl must remain firm in her faith when she, the mother, no longer lived.

Theresa was not yet five years old when her father again led her to the bedside of her mother, but this time the pale figure did not place her hand on the little head as she had always done. "She is dead," sobbed her father. Theresa did not understand this, but she knew that she had suffered a great loss. The dismal atmosphere frightened her; it was her first contact with grief.

No one could say who was more helpless—the lonely father or the bereaved children. They could not remain alone. It was self-evident, therefore, that the faithful aunt continue to take care of the house and the little ones. For five years she continued in self-sacrificing service until Mayor Pfaender came to her one day and said: "Become a true mother to my children and a wife to me as well." They were married, and eventually the number of children was increased by the birth of three boys. With this addition to the family, the work also increased. After school hours, Theresa was constantly cradling a little brother on her knees and watching the others at play. In this way she developed a sense of care and responsibility. Her second mother resembled her own mother in goodness, and piety, and Theresa observed what she told the little ones. In Theresa's diary we can read how she gradually lost interest in childish play and amusements, and how study and prayer brought her more and more joy.

Theresa always felt most at home in church and in school. She loved to be with the family but when she was at home, she was more and more frequently exposed to her father's vehement pressure to embrace his religion. Mr. Pfaender loved his eldest daughter with a special preference. She was quick-minded, prudent, and energetic, and in her he discovered his own characteristics. Moreover, she gave promise of being a good assistant in the management of his official duties. He could no longer bear it that they disagreed in this single point.

Theresa was now twelve years of age, and she was growing restless to be permitted to kneel at the Table of the Lord for the first time. It was customary to grant this privilege at the age of fourteen, but she requested her pastor, Reverend Ernst, and her father to permit her to attend the First Communion instructions before the required age. Both granted her request. Her father, however, granted it only under the condition that she simultaneously submit to religious instructions in *his* church in order to choose between the two beliefs.

The child knelt more frequently in church; her little heart was torn in discord. Which way should she follow? Should she obey her father? He certainly meant well, and after all, wasn't everything he did right? Or was her mother right when, shortly before her death, she made the sign of the cross on her forehead and said: "That is the sign of the Catholic faith; you must never forget what you have learned, my child."

Theresa listened to her interior voice—listened as she looked steadfastly toward the altar for an answer. And she did receive light. Very clearly she saw her way. We do not know whether her mother helped her from heaven, but the seed of faith, which the good woman had once planted in the heart of her child, bore its first beautiful blossom. Theresa resolved to remain Catholic. "I chose with full conviction," she writes, "and, after many hindrances and many persistent requests, I finally received the consent of my father and had the great happiness to receive Holy Communion on May 24, 1840."

During the severe afflictions of her childhood, Theresa found understanding and help in her second mother. In devoted love she clung to her, and her sorrow was unutterable when she stood for a second time at a deathbed. Again a bewildered father wrung his hands—eight children were now without a mother. Was he not forced to marry again? He did not hesitate very long. For the third time, he contracted marriage—this time with Theresa Brand; and again six times a child lay in the cradle.

In the meantime, the oldest daughter had well-nigh outgrown her school days. With a sad heart, she foresaw that this happy time would end shortly. At school she was in her element. She grasped everything she heard so quickly that she was a valuable assistant to her teacher, Miss Luecke, who entrusted the little ones to her. How wonderfully Theresa could get along with children! She had certainly had enough experience at home. But when she could truly be a teacher,

her heart swelled with joy. This was much nicer than playing school at home. Miss Luecke furthered the knowledge of her young assistant by private instructions and gave her courses in pedagogy and in methods.

Before her school days ended, Theresa had already discovered her vocation. She states: "More than happy to be a child of our holy Church and to have attained what I had sought with so much difficulty, I resolved, immediately after my First Holy Communion, to dedicate my time and strength to the welfare of youth, and therefore I asked my father for permission to embrace the teaching profession. He granted me permission to continue my studies but not for the teaching profession."

When Theresa had to leave her beloved school at the age of thirteen, Miss Luecke was able to give an excellent report of her. She stresses "her special inclination to the teaching profession," and praises "her outstanding intellectual abilities, her persevering diligence, her popularity with children, and her blossoming, deep, joyful, religious spirit." In a report, the Reverend Father Hundt, the local school inspector, remarks that in addition to her piety and meekness, "The young assistant teacher has achieved a more than usual intellectual and technical education through ability and diligence."

Theresa was allowed to attend a private night school to supplement and broaden her education. She gave all her attention to her studies. Even though her father endeavored to suppress her heart's desire by a curt refusal, she clung to it tenaciously. Who knows but that she might some day be permitted to be a teacher and an educator! This great desire urged her on toward this profession.

3

The call of the King

SOMETHING UNANTICIPATED SUDDENLY INTERRUPTED Theresa's secret yearning. Her father bade farewell to the beloved village of Hallenberg. There were many tears when he decided to change his place of residence and move with his large family to the nearby village of Liesen.

Hallenberg—Liesen. How entirely different life had become! No longer any school rooms with sparkling eyes of children, no further education under her esteemed teacher, no evening classes. Gone were the intimate hours spent at twilight in the old parish church. All this crushed her young heart and adjustment to her new environment was very difficult. Yet she welcomed the opportunity of helping her father in his office, and he soon discovered that he might confidently entrust his books to her, for Miss Luecke had not exaggerated when she gave her student good grades in neatness, diligence, arithmetic, and writing. Mr. Pfaender was proud of his eldest daughter; while Theresa likewise had no greater joy than to set her father at ease by her good work. All this must have softened his heart. But why was he really opposed to his daughter's wish? Had she not shown that she was really capable of guiding and teaching youth? Did he not see that? Or was he disturbed by a secret fear that the pious girl might recognize still another vocation along with the call to the teaching profession?

At any rate, he was certain that no secretary would work as well and as cheaply as his Theresa; therefore, it would be nonsensical to give her up. Was that not also the opinion of her pastor, Reverend Loeser? Let him express his ideas about the matter. He was indeed a good friend of the family and truly loved the children. He would be able to give advice.

But the pastor was also a man of whom the villagers said: "When he has a goal in mind, he will not be stopped." And that statement must have been true because he actually succeeded in convincing the adamant Mr. Pfaender that Theresa was far from having completed her education.

Did Mr. Pfaender really think that his daughter had quaffed sufficiently from the fountain of knowledge? Nonsense! Surely, the few sips Theresa had taken had certainly not quenched her thirst! Did he seriously believe that in his municipal office Theresa would learn all that she was still lacking? Most assuredly not! But he, the pastor, would gladly help her with her education and would furnish her with the necessary equipment for her vocation as a teacher.

How insistent indeed was this family friend! And it was not long before Theresa was on her way to the pastor's residence.

Father Loeser had not promised too much. Theresa was an apt pupil in cooking and sewing in the rectory. He himself was her teacher in the various branches of learning. Once more she was granted the joy of general classroom activity. Father Loeser had established a Sunday school and a choral class. Theresa did not have to be told to attend both. Over and above this, the pious and zealous priest knew only too well what his protege needed. His example and his word gave impetus to Theresa's growth in piety and virtue.

As she was once encouraged to help her father in his office, so she was now allowed to help the good pastor with his own clerical work. What she had learned by her contacts with businessmen and by drawing up documents was to her advantage now. Father Loeser, known to be extremely business minded, loved precision in all his work and in the records in his office. Father Loeser was quite happy to have Theresa relieve him of much work. He was still more pleased, however, by her modest behavior and her pious disposition. In this she resembled Regina, his little sister, who belonged to the pastor's household. Both girls were devoted to each other in deep friendship; and, what they anxiously concealed from strangers, they mutually entrusted to each other. Was not this routine spiritual life in the rectory a preparation for a similar life of their own? How they envied women religious who could devote themselves entirely to works of love and piety!

But the happy time in the rectory of Zueschen came to an abrupt end. In 1848, Father Loeser was called to Paderborn —called from the peace of his forest village to the office of Procurator at the episcopal seminary. Theresa returned home, to the joy of her father—he had dispensed with her help long enough—and to the great joy of her harassed foster mother, who was steeped in work. Now the grown-up daughter could help take care of the children again.

Theresa tried to do justice to all their wishes, both in her father's office and in the nursery. However, a decision had to be made concerning her future. Ever since her First Holy Communion, Theresa had become more and more conscious of the vocation that was present in her soul.

It was now necessary for her to fight a real battle with great courage. How was she to make her father understand that she not only felt urged to become a teacher but that she also wished to become a religious? There arose a persistent contention between father and daughter, which lasted for almost two years. Innumerable objections were the answer to Theresa's incessant plea. And again—as had happened in choosing her faith—with a bleeding heart, she struggled for a decision.

"Stay!" pleaded the father.

"Don't go away!" cried her brothers and sisters.

And another Voice called: "Listen, O daughter, and see, and incline your ear! Forget your people and your father's house; it is the King who desires your beauty."

4

An answer to the call

FINALLY, THERESA'S PRAYERS AND PERSISTENCE WON OUT. Her father finally gave his approval; however, Theresa must improve herself in domestic arts before she entered. These were his orders in spite of all her protests. Did he hope perhaps that further delay would change her mind? The place which Theresa chose for improving her domestic skills was certainly not one which would weaken her resolve. Father Loeser had remained her guide and spiritual director, and as Procurator of the seminary, he made it possible for her to obtain a position in the household of the seminary at Paderborn, beginning in January, 1850. How quickly she fell in love with the regular life, the solitude, and the atmosphere of the house!

Then there came the day of the decisive meeting with Pauline von Mallinckrodt, the Foundress of the Sisters of Christian Charity. As a petitioner, Theresa stood before the noble woman, who, after many difficulties, was wearing the religious garb for only one year and had gathered about herself a community of Sisters who dedicated themselves to works of charity and education.

Theresa requested admission into the young community and she was accepted. Mother Pauline was not too hasty in her acceptance of applicants to the community. In the first three years, only twenty-one out of fifty received admission into the novitiate. Theresa was among the fortunate.

Everything happened much quicker than she had anticipated. In June, 1850, she concluded her domestic activity in the seminary, and on July 4 the doors of the convent of the Sisters of Christian Charity opened to her. Her postulancy lasted five months. Pauline von Mallinckrodt was an excellent mother and mistress to the young candidate. On November 4, 1850, Theresa knelt before the Bishop of Paderborn, Doctor Francis Drepper. He gave her the holy habit and called her, for the first time, by her new name as a religious—Sister Clara.

5

A new call

THE INVESTITURE DID NOT INITIATE THE USUAL YEAR OF
seclusion. Since Mother Pauline had very few Sisters, she
could not afford to keep her novices in the solitude of the little
Motherhouse. They were sent to the missions immediately.
"To Dortmund," thus did Sister Clara's first obedience read,
"as helper to an experienced Sister in an elementary and sewing school."

"I am fortunate to belong to a community which dedicates
itself to the education and instruction of youth," Sister Clara
joyfully admitted. Yes, she was again in her element. How
well God had ordained everything! After years filled with
anxiety over the choice of her vocation, she enjoyed peace of
heart for the first time. Moreover, she was grateful when she
received good news from home, too, for everybody was finally
resigned to her religious vocation. If only God would grant
her father, the father of a large family of children, a long life.

She could scarcely believe it when the news came that he
was dead.

Only from a distance could Sister Clara console her poor
mother and her many brothers and sisters. However, in the
midst of all this sorrow God himself had given wondrous
consolation. Her father had embraced the Catholic faith be-

fore his death. Might she not perceive in this great grace a
little fruit of her own incessant prayers for him? Her happiness had been completed by his recent approval of her choice
of vocation, even though it was given only after great inner
turmoil.

Mother Pauline soon recognized that the zealous novice
was in her right place with the children, for Sister Clara's
resolute and confident approach made her especially capable
of managing boys.

A new obedience came: "To Steele, as educator for seventy
adolescent orphan boys." The young Sister was not afraid of
this assignment. Three years later the director of the orphanage was able to send a praiseworthy testimony to the
Motherhouse. "Sister Clara has fulfilled the duties assigned
to her with much insight and knowledge and with unusual
diligence and indefatigable zeal to the greatest satisfaction of
her Superiors. Although she strictly insisted on order and unconditional obedience, she nevertheless won and constantly
maintained the esteem, love, affection, and the unconditional
trust of her pupils through her kind treatment and attention."

The young religious was in the convent scarcely four years,
having taken her temporary vows on February 17, 1853,
when she was appointed Superior of the mission in Solingen
together with the office of Principal of the elementary and
sewing school. When she was later transferred, Reverend
Saenger, the local inspector of schools, reported: "She possesses great skill in teaching and so easily wins the good will
of the children by her unusual approach that they all love
her sincerely."

Sister Clara's obvious teaching aptitude was still to be used
to its greatest extent. She was given the care and education of
blind children in an institute for the blind at Paderborn.
When a finishing course was begun for candidates for pro-
fessional teaching at the Motherhouse in 1856, Sister Clara

Pfaender was enrolled. Wholeheartedly, she devoted herself to her studies. Her congregation was justified in expecting great success from her because of her character and her pedagogical and social qualifications.

During the course of the seminar, Mother Pauline had been planning to send the young teacher to another mission— to Witten as Superior and Principal of the elementary school. She could not possibly have known that a turbulent struggle had arisen in the heart of her daughter. Sister Clara had repeatedly asserted she was happy in her calling as a teacher and an educator. Therefore, no one surmised that for three years she had been harassed by doubts of being in the right place.

More and more her thoughts reverted to the days of her youth with their daily hours of adoration in the old parish church. Was it not there that she had first become aware that such adoration should be her life's task? Undoubtedly, her religious day was now completely dedicated to prayer and works of love for youth, but the interior call could not be silenced—the call to lead a stricter mode of life and to impose as a duty, before all others, the adoration of the Most Blessed Sacrament.

Her studies, however, must not suffer under this anguish of soul. The time for the final examination drew near; and on July 17, 1858, Theresa Pfaender received the certificate from the Royal Examining Committee.

Should she now open her heart to good Mother Pauline? But surely that would be unprincipled just at this time! And was it truly God who had caused this disquietude? Or was it the devil—the disturber of all peace? Hundreds of times she had pondered how she could express herself. Hesitation grew to martyrdom. One day, with a sudden determination, she rose quickly from prayer and knocked at Mother Pauline's door.

Sister Clara had hoped that she would find understanding, but she had scarcely dreamed of so much kindness and such readiness to be of assistance. There was not a word of pressure to remain; not the least reproach that she had just completed her studies and that the community was waiting for her. Instead, Mother Pauline manifested heartfelt sympathy for the one who was about to leave her community.

This noble woman wanted nothing for herself; everything, however, for the honor of God, even if he should demand the giving back of a child in whom she had placed great hope. With the consoling assurance that she would help her, Mother Pauline dismissed the troubled Sister.

A glance toward the crucifix; a fervent quest for counsel in prayer; then line after line appeared in a letter from Mother Pauline's trembling hands:

Paderborn, August 16, 1858

Very Reverend Mother:

A Sister of our community believes that she has a decided calling to a stricter Order; and since admission into a stricter Order is permitted by Holy Church, I do not wish to hinder her from carrying it out. Therefore, I ask leave to inquire whether perhaps she might find admission with you. Permit me to enclose the respective report of the Reverend Director of the seminary together with other papers. In July, of this year, she passed her teacher's examination. In a short time I shall receive the results of this examination from the government. She is exceptionally pious, possesses an excellent gift of attracting children, and has a pleasant disposition. She does not possess wealth, but I think her educational background will compensate for it.

I earnestly request that you kindly give me a short reply or return the papers within a few days, since the matter is urgent. I must know if we are going to lose her or if I should give her some activity in our community.

In case you accept her, may I request that it take place immediately. She would hand over personally a document from our most worthy Bishop, in which he approves her transfer from our community to your Order.

Four times Mother Pauline wrote this letter: To the Franciscans in Heydthausen, Holland; to the Sisters of Perpetual Adoration in Bonn; to the Poor Clares in Muenster, and to the Trappistines in Oelenberg, Alsace.

Almost immediately the replies came in: The Trappistines refused, because their convent had too many members already. The Poor Clares refused for the same reason, adding that they occupied themselves only with prayer and with house and garden work, and had no employment for a teacher. The Franciscans at Heydthausen and the Sisters of Perpetual Adoration were not against admitting Sister Clara. Yet for the present she remained in the community. In prayer and waiting, she submitted to the will of God.

Then for the first time she felt the urge to call into being a community whose members would devote themselves, above all, to perpetual adoration of the Most Blessed Sacrament, to prayer for our persecuted holy Church, and to the performance of works of Christian charity. She was permitted at that time to receive Holy Communion daily. Suddenly every doubt vanished; she knew—"That is my way!"

Once more she sought the help of Mother Pauline and begged her for permission to communicate her inner thoughts to the Bishop of Paderborn.

That would have been easy for her if the kindly Bishop, Doctor Francis Drepper, were still alive. Mother Pauline had known this fatherly protector of the community very well. It was only recently that his successor, Doctor Conrad Martin, occupied the episcopal throne. True, he was said to be favorably disposed to religious; however, he was not yet well-known to the Sisters of Christian Charity.

Had her interior call not been so emphatic, Sister Clara would never have found the courage to go to the Bishop's residence. However, in a trembling voice, she, who was ordinarily not lost for words, submitted her request to the

Prince of the Church. While she spoke hesitatingly, her customary troubled thoughts arose again. What? She wanted
that—she, Theresa Pfaender, the inexperienced girl from the
mountains of southern Westphalia? How could she be guide
and Mother of perhaps many hundreds or even thousands!
Would she not rather be subject to a Mother than be a
Mother?

However, she had now spoken the momentous words.
Bishop Conrad Martin's look rested calmly and fatherly on
the young Sister at his feet. She no longer stood, for she had
long since sunk to her knees, a picture of dependency and of
trustful pleading: "Please help me so that I may obtain the
necessary insight for this task. Tell me what to do!"

She had not noticed how the Bishop's eyes shone at her
modest question as to whether such a foundation for that type
of activity could be established in his bishopric.

Furthermore, how should Sister Clara know that, ever since
his assuming of this high position of the call of God, he had
felt within himself the desire to obtain a community of pious
women in his diocese who would offer all their works for our
persecuted holy Church. Since then he had knelt countless
hours in the quiet of the night before the Tabernacle of his
private chapel and had prayed both for light to know how to
solve this problem and for an indication of the opportune time.

Was this the solution? Was now the time? The Bishop
folded his hands. He betrayed nothing whatever of his
thoughts, but joy and gratitude filled his heart. When Sister
Clara begged to be allowed to complete her avowal in the
Sacrament of Penance, he was immediately ready to hear her
confession.

His word gave her peace and encouragement. She should
for the time being remain confidently in her accustomed way
and let God provide. So far God had only lightly laid His
hand upon her; she would soon perceive when this hand would

stretch forth challengingly: Now is the time! Go and begin!

Gratefully, Sister Clara followed his fatherly counsel. Several times subsequently she knelt in the confessional of her Episcopal Director. Very soon the pious shepherd knew: "This is the tool with which I am to carry out God's order."

"You will recognize God's challenge," the Bishop had said. Therefore, Sister Clara was not in too great a hurry and willingly allowed herself to be sent to the previously assigned duty.

On September 14, 1858, her government diploma qualified her for the teaching profession; immediately the young teacher traveled to Witten. In the elementary school, teaching was not difficult for her; and for the convent she was a prudent and motherly Superior.

Along with her work in school and her religious obligations as Superior, she had ample time to remain quietly in the presence of God. Through these intimate conversations with God she gradually recognized clearly what God wanted of her.

6

New answer and new name

SISTER CLARA HAD SPENT ALMOST A DECADE IN THE COM-
munity of the Sisters of Christian Charity. The time spent in
study and in practical work had given her scarcely any opportunity to become acquainted with young women in the
world, whom she might approach for the fulfillment of her
plan.

One alone stood out clearly before Sister Clara's eyes, day
and night, as she sought counsel in prayer—Regina Loeser,
her dearest friend in the rectory at Zueschen. For some time
Regina had lived in her parental home at Olpe. Could there
be a better companion than she for the foundation? How
often they had exchanged their pious wishes and half-formu-
lated plans! Life had separated them in space; but in their
hearts they had remained close friends. Yes, Regina was the
very one who should be won for the new undertaking.

A friendly invitation brought Regina to Witten. She did
not come alone. For a long time she had been a close friend
of Aline Bonzel, the oldest daughter of a well-to-do merchant
in Olpe. Both had felt the call to the religious life for a long
time. With astonishment and enthusiasm, they listened to the
unexpected news that Sister Clara had to tell them. Regina
was immediately inclined to say, "Yes." Aline hesitated, al-

though she promised that she would gladly support the new
project financially. Its beginnings were too serious to be rushed.

The advice of a priest who was related to Regina Loeser
strengthened her in the resolution to join Sister Clara. He
likewise dispelled Aline Bonzel's remaining doubts, although
her uncle impressively warned against a foundation in Olpe
because another community was already actively engaged in
works of charity there.

Once more the three chosen ones found themselves together
in Witten. There thorough discussion resulted in the determination to found a congregation with the purpose, "To
benefit holy Mother Church by zealous prayer in a life of
perfection and to devote oneself to the care and welfare of
poor neglected orphans."

Since there was no one present in the little chapel, the two
friends knelt on either side of Sister Clara before the Tabernacle to make a quiet holy hour, before they returned home.
With ready hearts, the three bowed their heads deeply and
spoke a threefold *Fiat*. This was the beginning of a new
holy life.

God had sown the seed.

It was not a surprise for Pauline von Mallinckrodt, in late
summer of 1859, to receive a letter postmarked Witten, in
which Sister Clara asked to be released as soon as possible to
take up her new task. Neither did Bishop Conrad Martin need
a profuse explanation when requested to approve her departure from the Community of the Sisters of Christian Charity.

On September 9, 1859, Mother Pauline informed Sister
Clara that the Bishop had granted his approval. She might
leave Witten on September 20, and on September 23, she
could travel to Olpe. A few days in Paderborn would serve to
complete arrangements of matters pertaining to both sides and
would give her time for an audience with His Excellency, the

Bishop. Mother Pauline advised in a friendly way that Sister Clara leave Witten as quietly as possible so as to avoid giving rise to undesirable talk.

Yes, the counsel of Mother Pauline was good—as quietly as possible! However, it soon became known why Sister Clara was being called away. How difficult were the ten days she had to endure before her departure! How much lighter was her heart ten years before as she packed her trunk to follow her first call! At that time her future had looked bright with the certainty of being relieved of all personal care. She would follow a path according to God's will; a Mother, to whom she would be deeply united through obedience, would guide her.

And today? Apart from the calling and the *Fiat,* nothing is clear as yet. The way and the manner are clothed in darkness.

On the appointed day, a trembling hand rang the bell of the Motherhouse of the Sisters of Christian Charity, just as long ago at her happy *Introibo.*

And yet—how different! Now the door was being opened: Entrance—for exit! The two stood facing each other—Mother Pauline and Sister Clara. Mothers of many spiritual daughters: the one, already marked as Mother by the painful conception of her office; the other—

Pauline von Mallinckrodt removed most of the bitterness of this difficult hour by her goodness and noble bearing. As she led Theresa Pfaender to the cloister door two days later, both bowed to each other in mute departure. The Lord wanted it thus! With a silent handshake the one expressed her deepest gratitude; the other, her motherly blessing.

In the archives of the convent the name "Sister Clara" was deleted from the list of the Sisters of Christian Charity. That was September 23, 1859.

The early autumn wind had new strength. It swept the streets and drove the people before it. The simply dressed

woman who had just emerged from the convent at the War-
burger Tor lost herself in the crowd. She walked out with
confidence. It was still early morning.

How could Theresa now have any other destination than
the nearby church! It was not far to the Franciscans. Only a
few devout souls were in the church. She sank down into the
old oaken pew and buried her tear-moistened face in her
hands. Her mind was empty of thought. No word except
"Fiat!" escaped her lips.

She knelt in the confessional and then at the Communion
rail. As the faithful left the church after Mass, she arose and
was admitted to the Third Order of St. Francis by the aged
priest who had heard her confession. The first happy smile
lit up her countenance when, with fervent emphasis, the kind
old priest called her "Sister Clara" as a daughter of St. Francis.

7

"A sower went out to sow his seed" *Mark 4:3*

Sister Clara remained in devout prayer for some time. Then she knelt erect, and with decision she arose. She must now take direct steps toward her goal—God's pastures. The seed she carried well preserved in her heart.

In the market place the postilion was blowing his horn. In a short time Sister Clara was sitting between the chattering travelers in the high-wheeled mail coach. "To Olpe!" she answered to the coachman's inquiry as to her destination. An entire night and day passed by before she arrived early Saturday morning in the little city located deep down in southern Westphalia.

How Regina Loeser and Aline Bonzel had longed for her presence! It had not been easy to obtain an understanding and an approval for the "leap into uncertainty" from father and mother. Now that all misgivings had been removed, their only wish was that their plan might soon become a reality.

With great joy, therefore, they received her whom they had awaited. Their first visit was to the Most Blessed Sacrament in the parish church. Only a few weeks had elapsed since they knelt before the Tabernacle in Witten after their important deliberation and bowed their heads in a three-fold *Fiat*. Now the three knelt again before the altar, lifted their

heads joyfully, spoke a sincere *Deo Gratias* for their preliminary steps, and asked God's blessing on their future.

After exchanging friendly greetings with the Loeser and
Bonzel families, the three companions eventually found a
little time for themselves. Just two days before, on September
22, Clara Pfaender had sent a petition to Bishop Conrad
Martin to obtain for her and her companions the permission
to carry out their magnanimous resolve. She now presented
this important document to the other two. With hands folded
as if in prayer, they read:

Most Reverend Bishop:
   May it please Your Excellency that I present you in a spirit
of holy reverence and deepest submission the following:
   Having spent nine contented years in the Community of the
Sisters of Christian Charity and having joyfully expended
strength of body and soul in the service of the blind and especially in the education of youth, I have felt for several years
the call to a stricter and a more perfect life for the greater
honor of God and the salvation of souls.
   As a result, after incessant prayer and mature consideration,
I have several times requested my Superiors for permission to
leave this congregation, so dear to me, and I have received this
permission from them after much deliberation. It is now my
sincerest desire to follow the manifest call of God; to lead a
perfect religious life united with several pious, like-minded
young ladies; to aid by zealous prayer our holy Catholic Church;
and to care for poor, neglected orphans.
   We desire in accordance with the holy will of God to offer
up our poor prayers for the spread of our holy Church, for the
Holy Father, for bishops, priests, and especially for all the
clergy; furthermore, for the conversion of sinners, of heretics
and unbelievers, and for the poor souls; but in a special manner
to pray and to offer sacrifices for our very highly esteemed
Bishop and his beloved diocese.
   We likewise desire with sincere devotion and love to honor the
Most Sacred Heart of Jesus and the Immaculate Heart of Mary
and to promote this devotion as much as we can in the present
age.

Simultaneously, we would like to serve our Divine Lord primarily in the care of poor, abandoned orphans and to dedicate our talents to their instructions and education.

Profoundly aware of our nothingness, we place our whole trust in Almighty God, who is indeed strong in his weak ones and who will be our helper and our supporter by his all-powerful grace.

In order, however, to be most closely united with our holy Church, we request Your Excellency to take us under your episcopal protection. In the name of Jesus and Mary, we present our request in deepest humility and await with confident trust that Your Excellency will grant permission to carry out this holy plan and bestow upon us your episcopal blessing.

In deepest reverence and submission, Your Excellency, I am,

Your most lowly servant,
Theresa Clara Pfaender

That was essentially the plan as formulated in Witten. With great joy and satisfaction these companions listened to the answer which their Bishop had written immediately after receiving their letter:

To Miss Theresa Clara Pfaender:

To your petition on the twenty-second of this month, allow me to say that from my point of view, I cannot recall anything against the plan which you have made known to me, namely, of leading a secluded life with several pious young ladies and of caring for poor orphans according to your ability, with the understanding that, in your undertaking, you will at all times be led by the spirit of genuine piety as well as by the rules of Christian prudence.

I must, however, make my episcopal approval of your work dependent upon your fulfilling the guarantees requested by the Church for a successful continuation of such a form of life in the future.

Paderborn, September 22, 1859.

(Signed) ✠ Bishop Conrad

The Bishop's letter passed from hand to hand; then Clara Pfaender folded it together, made a sign of the cross on it, and placed it carefully into the little metal safety box. It was the cornerstone of her congregation.

The following days entailed important visits with the pastor and with the mayor of the place. Both were keenly interested in the foundation of a new community and of an orphanage, and they promised their assistance.

The three co-founders had previously decided not to organize community life too rapidly. They wanted to prepare themselves for their work by a week of reflection and prayer. Since there was no opportunity for this at Olpe, they traveled to Aix-la-Chapelle, for they had often heard rumors that here exemplary religious life was in full bloom. After six days they arrived on October 4th in the old imperial city. With the Sisters of the Poor Child Jesus they found a loving reception and were able to prepare their hearts for their great task by making a retreat of several days with them.

Mother Francisca Schervier, the Foundress of the Poor Sisters of St. Francis, also gladly espoused the cause of these three who sought counsel. She was indefatigable in imparting to them words of wisdom and direction from her varied experiences, and she presented them with the Marian Office before they left. Happy and proud, they received this Office as the first item of their religious equipment. Enriched with many practical words of advice, they returned home.

In the meantime a modest dwelling had been acquired in Olpe for the three chosen ones. The Bonzel family and several other friendly families considered it a point of honor to be able to offer them their first home. The little house of widow Schuerholz lay in the vicinity of the parish church. There the members of the little religious family took up residence after they had returned from their fatiguing trip.

These pious women were not yet bound by the vow of poverty. However, they had many opportunities to practice this favorite virtue of St. Francis. The furnishings of their small dwelling were meager; their food, scanty; and their straw mattress, hard; yet the hearts of these carefree women rejoiced. They entrusted themselves to the Providence of God. It was not long before young ladies, who had heard of their plans, knocked at the door and begged admittance to their number. Sister Clara tested their desire and then gladly accepted them. The more the number increased, the more abundantly did alms flow into the house. These alms were also sufficient to support the first four orphans, who were under their care.

The daily schedule of prayer, work, and recreation followed the plan drafted by Sister Clara and approved by the Bishop. The number, three, had already tripled; and all looked upon Sister Clara as a Mother and Mistress. That meant it was up to her to provide shelter, food, and drink; she gave instructions in catechism and asceticism; she was the teacher of the orphans; and finally it was she who had to draft the Constitutions.

When her companions wanted to know what was to be done and what omitted, they only had to turn to Sister Clara. She was their leader and their still unwritten rule. By her example, all could recognize the pattern by which she wished her community to be known. Mother Pauline had once written of her daughter: "She is exceptionally pious, has the gift of attracting children to her in a high degree, and has a pleasant appearance." Were not these the virtues of a foundress? Sister Clara was to those who followed her a model both in prayer and in works of charity.

Since their first dwelling had been too small for quite some time, they moved into a larger house in the early part of the year. Sister Clara and her companions still wore secular clothing. How long the year of trial, which the Bishop had ordered, seemed! It ended September 23, 1860. A holy contest in religious striving united the nine. "Make yourselves worthy of your calling," was Sister Clara's daily exhortation.

By August, Sister Clara had already sent the statutes and the outline for investiture to Paderborn. On September 29th she entrusted to the mail coach three thick sealed letters: one from each of her companions, Aline Bonzel and Regina Loeser, and a third written by herself. They were addressed to His Excellency, the Most Reverend Bishop Dr. Conrad Martin, and bore similar contents—a request for the approval of the statutes and for their investiture in the near future. Two letters contained a noteworthy postscript: "Truly holy is the life of our fellow-sister, Sister Clara. Therefore, we request that you appoint her Superior of our young community."

In the meantime, they prayed devoutly. When would the answer arrive? With growing concern, Sister Clara looked for a message on those days on which the postilion sounded his horn.

And when this letter did not arrive, a slight twitching of her countenance betrayed how difficult it was for her to preserve patience, for her quick temperament looked for immediate action. She forced herself to retain her composure, so that, when she entered the sewing room a little later, none of the busy seamstresses saw a trace of impatience in her attitude.

Nine brown habits were already prepared, cut in the form of a cross out of coarse material. Nine black scapulars were in readiness, having two hearts encircled by a crown of stars above a monogram and a cross stitched in red.

Nine white cords were likewise made by the skilled fingers of the women. Sister Clara had learned the art of making the knots from Mother Francisca Schervier. The last stitches were being put into the white linen coifs, and devout activity reigned in the small sewing room. Their hands moved briskly, but only the pearly song of the joyful rosary broke the silence.

8

"Light and darkness, praise the Lord" *Dan. 3:72*

THE LONGER THE POSTULANTS HAD TO WAIT, THE MORE devout became their prayers; and the more zealous, their striving after virtue. Now it scarcely ever happened that the parish church was empty at twilight. Whether in the morning, when a child tripped lightly over the grey stone slabs of the wide floors, or toward evening, when the cane of an old man gently tapped the floor, there was always an adorer there in the stillness of God's house. The people became accustomed to the sight of a devout woman kneeling in prayer in the first pew close to the altar. At the stroke of every hour from the old tower clock, a second lady would kneel down beside her and, with the quiet greeting: "Praised be Jesus Christ!" she would relieve the first from her hour of adoration.

For quite some time these pious women, who wanted to become Sisters, had followed this program of prayer. From morning to night they took turns in adoring the Blessed Sacrament. This alternating in prayer was to be the fundamental characteristic of Sister Clara's community: "For our holy Church and her shepherds," as she had once told the Bishop. Now that day by day she and her associates awaited more longingly his approval to the statutes of their community, there entered into their prayers for the Church the earnest request that God enlighten that shepherd under whose care they had placed themselves.

After a painful delay, Sister Clara finally held the answer of the Bishop in her hands. What would be its contents? As impatient as her waiting had been, so disciplined was her delay now in opening the letter. Pressing it against her rapidly beating heart, she knelt before the cross in their oratory. "Lord, Thy will be done!—no matter what the answer may be!" Then she broke the seal and read:

> Examined, and the use of the enclosed rule is approved.
> Paderborn, October 30, 1860.
>
> (Signed) ✠ Bishop Conrad

A blessed sense of relief ran through the body of the one kneeling. "You, O Lord, have blessed your people." She remained in prayer for a short time; then, quickly arose and sounded the bell. From all directions, her associates hastened to her side: from kitchen, basement, sewing room.

What had happened? What an absurd question! Sister Clara's eyes told them enough. They all sank to their knees and thanked God.

Together with the approval of the rule, Bishop Conrad Martin also sent the name for the new community:

Franciscan Sisters
Daughters of the Sacred Hearts
of Jesus and Mary

Thus the decision was made: they would become a religious community of the Third Order of St. Francis.

Sister Clara had at first wanted to make the rule of St. Augustine, which she had learned and loved, the basis of their common life. However, while she was staying at Aix-la-Chapelle, she felt drawn to follow in the footsteps of St. Francis. That is why she chose the Franciscan garb as the habit for her community, and yet there was always some interior resistance that opposed her abandoning the long-used Augustinian Rule. Now the Bishop clearly pointed out the way. Sister Clara and her associates gladly complied.

Dean Goerdes from the nearby town of Drolshagen, appointed as the first Reverend Superior of the community, was able to report to the Bishop toward the end of November that he had conscientiously examined the nine candidates and considered them worthy to receive the holy habit.

Soon he received the episcopal commission to arrange with the community the day for the investiture. He himself would perform the ceremonies in the name of the Bishop, and upon their completion he would install Sister Clara as Superior.

This news was a source of extremely great joy to those waiting. After a short consultation, it was decided that the investiture take place on Thursday, December 20, which day would be very appropriate, because Thursday, the memorial day of the institution of the Holy Eucharist, should always remind the Sisters that their chief task is Eucharistic Adoration.

That was a holy Advent! Only a short time remained to dispatch external business matters. Then in silence and recollection, all prepared themselves for the holy event. Sister Clara lectured to her associates during the retreat. With the love of a mother, she explained how they were to walk in the path of perfection, according to the will of God. Her words found easy access into their hearts, and all reiterated: "My heart is ready, O Lord, my heart is ready!"

Houses and streets were decorated as the nine happy young ladies, led by the clergy and accompanied by many faithful of the city, made their way to the church on December 20. Olpe had never experienced such a celebration. In his sermon the Reverend Superior Goerdes placed this new project into the hands of God to show that it was established in him.

The bells rang out joyfully as the little flock, clothed in the brown robe of St. Francis and girded with a white cord, was led back to the convent. Sister Clara came last. She knew that, before all others, she was most closely united to the Seraphic Father—today she was given the name of his most beloved daughter for the third time, together with the title which designated her by name as the Mother of all the Daughters of the Sacred Hearts of Jesus and Mary to whom the community was consecrated.

Theresa Pfaender was now called Sister Mary Clara of the Sacred Hearts of Jesus and Mary.

Aline Bonzel received the name Sister Mary Theresa of the Most Blessed Sacrament; and Regina Loeser became Sister Mary Anthony of the Immaculate Conception.

The Sisters assembled in the convent oratory where Reverend Superior Goerdes read the episcopal decree which made Sister Clara their Superior for a two-year term. Now they constituted a real community. Each one came up individually, knelt down, and kissed Sister Clara's hand as a sign of recognition of her office and as a public profession of obedience.

This day of consecration to God was not to be disturbed by an external celebration. It ended in recollection and prayer. A new day of joy was in the offing. Bishop Conrad Martin had sent his greatest gift on this occasion—his permission to keep the Most Blessed Sacrament in their oratory. On the morning of December 1, the Eucharistic King made his entrance into their little sanctuary. All hearts were filled with overwhelming gratitude.

Mother Clara and Sister Anthony were deeply touched when Reverend Loeser approached the altar to celebrate Holy Mass. Before their eyes stood the rectory of Zueschen, the birthplace of their religious vocation. What their priestly brother and friend saw secretly developing and blossoming in both young girls years ago and what he lovingly fostered, he was now permitted to see beautifully crowned.

The Lord had set up his abode in their midst. Now it was fitting that he receive the tribute of adoration. Immediately after the *Ite, Missa est!* Mother Clara knelt before the Tabernacle and officially began the prayer for the oppressed holy Church and her shepherds. "Never, as long as the community exists, should this service before the Most Blessed Sacrament come to an end!" she vowed in the name of her daughters.

Heaven seemed very close. What God once said of the magnificent temple at Jerusalem was now more appropriate for the poor little chapel with its tabernacle: "For I have chosen and have sanctified this place, that my name may be there forever; and my eyes and my heart may remain there perpetually" (2 Par. 7, 16).

Then began the ordinary routine in the convent of the Francisan Sisters, Daughters of the Sacred Hearts of Jesus and Mary. In Mother Clara's explanation of this name, she gave a striking ascetical directive: "The community . . . endeavors, in accordance with the example of our Divine Savior and his holy Mother Mary, to unite the contemplative and active life so that the latter be nourished, strengthened, and supported by the former, and thereby become more richly blessed."

Prayer and work mutually combined—thus bade the first challenge of their conventual life. How much it meant to Mother Clara, that her Sisters be a group of zealous adorers for the oppressed Church, is evident in the introduction to her statutes:

> The Franciscan Sisters, Daughters of the Sacred Hearts of Jesus and Mary, have united in holy love for the greater honor and glory of God so that by continual prayer they might especially aid our holy Catholic Church in her struggles and persecutions. Therefore, the Sisters, as victims of the Divine Heart of Jesus, oblige themselves to offer up daily all their prayers, works

of penance, Holy Masses, Holy Communions—in short all good works which they perform with the help of God's grace. In the Motherhouse they will take turns, day and night, in presenting the incense of their humble and ardent prayers to the love-inflamed Heart of Jesus, hidden in the Most Blessed Sacrament, for our Holy Father; for all bishops, priests, and religious—especially for the clergy in general; further for the conversion of sinners, heretics, and infidels; for their charges, relatives, and benefactors; for the sick and the dying; and for the poor souls in purgatory.

And what did Mother Clara plan regarding the active apostolate in the community? As a special object of her foundation she undertook: "Care, education, and instruction of youth; care of the poor sick in hospitals and homes . . . and above all the performance of all works of mercy as they arise."

The Sisters' "Labora," service of youth and service to the sick, should be in addition to their "Ora." In connection with this, Mother Clara was thinking foremost of the training of children in orphanages:

> The Sisters shall impart a complete elementary education to all children admitted to their homes, shall train them in needlework, and shall give them practice in the performance of domestic duties. Their charges may not be dismissed until they have received sufficient elementary education, made their First Holy Communion, and are in a position to earn their own livelihood. When the Sisters release their charges, they will endeavor to procure for them an occupation which will be favorable to the children's moral welfare in the world. They will keep them in mind as their children and support them at all times with counsel and help.

During the year of the Sisters' probation, four orphans were admitted—girls only on account of lack of space; but it was already planned that the Sisters devote themselves to the education and instruction of boys, when the possibilities seemed opportune.

As benevolent teaching Sisters, therefore, the daughters of

Mother Clara were to serve orphans in a spiritual motherhood.

But works of charity are without bounds. Therefore, in addition to the care of youth, the motherly vision of the Foundress saw a vast field of corporal and spiritual works of mercy for the sick. She decreed:

> Those Sisters who are scheduled neither for adoration nor for teaching will undertake to the best of their ability the nursing care of the poor sick in their homes and will serve God in them with Christ-like love.

Thus, the Sisters perform a threefold service:
Perpetual adoration,
Education and formation of youth,
Nursing care of the sick.

Nursing care had not been planned originally; however, it happened quite naturally that the Sisters were called on to attend the sick.

During the first months the poor daughters of St. Francis had acquired many benefactors. The good people came in the secrecy of the night and placed food and drink at the door of the convent. Others invited them to come and help themselves to whatever they needed.

In these quests for alms the Sisters came upon a sick person here and an invalid there in the houses of their benefactors. How consoling for such was the comforting word and the soothing hand! Thus it happened that the Sisters were soon called for a second and a third time, not only for the sake of receiving the alms, which their benefactors desired to place in their baskets, but also for the benefit of the treasured assistance the Sisters could bestow.

Before long, the door bell of the convent often rang at night to summon a Sister to the bedside of a sick person in distress. Could Mother Clara refuse her help? Should she have said: "There are other Sisters here; go to the hospital and seek help there?"

Should she have considered whether she needed permission to perform this type of charity? Did the good Samaritan ask himself whether he had the approval of the authorities before he ministered to the man cruelly beaten on the road to Jericho? Mother Clara did not think long about it. The Sisters responded to the call, helped, and promised to come again. However, an obstacle was placed in the way of their returning. Loud voices were raised: "The new Sisters should devote themselves to works of piety and the care of orphans, but they should not perform the other works of Christian charity—the care of the sick and the poor."

Did the board of directors of the hospital see in the home-visits of the sick, made by the Franciscans, an encroachment on the rights of the hospital?

Yes, and with every successive report of a home-visit, objections increased. These people did not hesitate to tell Mother Clara to restrict her works of charity to her own sphere of activity. Letters of complaint were sent to the Chancery stating that the home-visits of the sick endangered the rights of the hospital Sisters, who had been established there first. Even before the investiture, the town-councillor, moved by this concern, had warned the Bishop against approving the new foundation in Olpe, giving as a reason that the city was too small for the existence of two convents.

A group of citizens in the city council had the same apprehension; others were not worried. It was not long until the young community became the center of controversial opinions. Mother Clara suffered; and her daughters, likewise. They had come there to pray and to serve. Now they were restrained from performing the service of love. What was to be done?

Very quietly and unobtrusively they responded to occasional requests to visit the sick or dying. The glow of gratitude in the eyes of their patients was their sole thanks. In the background, there lurked chiefly the reproach that they were "not competent" for their service.

Soon it became customary in the Sisters' little convent to remember not only their benefactors in their evening prayer but also those who were making life difficult for them by their animosity. Yes, Mother Clara considered these also among her benefactors, and rightfully so.

As the attacks increased, she wrote to her Episcopal Patron:

> I see in these trials, battles and difficulties a solid foundation for our community. The more I appear to be deprived of all human support the more firmly and solidly do I establish the anchor of my hope in the Lord, in accordance with whose holy will and for whose greater honor I have undertaken so difficult a task. Surely, he supports the weak and will protect his cause.

Nothing could disturb the equanimity of this strong woman and her trust in God. In every situation she asked herself: "What does God want now?" She scarcely seemed to need human counsel. Was not everyone directed to seek God's counsel? She acted calmly and in accordance with the enlightenment which she acquired by prayerful reflection. Man might construe it as inordinate self-reliance, perhaps as self-willed assurance on her part, but that did not disturb her.

Had the time of oppression now come which was to prove whether the work was of God? "If it is of him, then it will endure," Reverend Superior Goerdes had said at the investiture. However, must it, under any cirumstances, continue to exist where it had been established? Or could the twig be transplanted? God's harvest field is large, and his seed can ripen fully everywhere.

Bishop Conrad Martin had seriously considered whether Olpe should become the first home of the young religious. From the very beginning he was inclined to recommend a different dwelling place to Mother Clara. Now that conflicts arose as a result of the requests for nursing care, he urgently advised the Sisters to leave Olpe. His letter of April 18, 1861, could not remain unheeded:

> Beloved Daughters in Christ!
> I have carefully examined the complaints against your community, which have arisen in Olpe. The complaint that you have appropriated the care of the sick in their homes, I cannot consider valid.
> On the other hand, sad to say, I am aware that even though your community should give no occasion for dissension, there will, nevertheless, continue to be disputes and from these irreparable scandals . . .
> I assure you that I cherish your community with sincere episcopal benevolence, and I shall at all times support it; however, because I sincerely wish your community well, I would not like to see it, even though innocent, be an occasion for scandalous disputes . . .
> I ask you, therefore, out of love for Jesus Christ, that you make the sacrifice for our dear God: either of removing your Motherhouse from Olpe to another place or at least of desisting from nursing the sick in Olpe. I know how difficult both of these will be for you, for it hurts my episcopal heart itself immeasurably to have to decide; however, the more difficult the sacrifice will be for you so much the greater will be the merit, so much the richer the blessing that will rest on your community . . .

Mother Clara dared not keep this message of the Bishop from her daughters. The news was bitter, especially for the Sisters from Olpe, since the convent lived chiefly on the benefactions of their native city. Above all others, it was the families related to the Sisters who vied with one another in doing good to the convent; and the financial and material support of many other citizens had been so profuse only because the convent was the pride of the city. Of what interest to them was a Motherhouse just anywhere in the world?

Now anxiety had really taken hold of the poor Franciscans. Mother Clara's heart did not hold out. Within a few weeks she was lying sick in bed. Her condition became so serious that all feared for her life. Sister Theresa, Mother's assistant, provided for the orphans and the convent with prudent deliberation and saw to it that her dear sick patient had the best of care. Weak and listless, Mother Clara lay on her narrow bed. Perhaps, she would soon exchange it for a still narrower one. To her weeping daughters, little hope remained.

Untiringly, Sister Anthony kept watch at the bedside of the sick one. She granted herself no rest day or night. The slightest motion revealed to Sister Anthony's eye how she might alleviate her patient's suffering. Her hand was gentle and gracious in everything she did. A grateful glance from her patient rewarded her every touch.

Scarcely a word passed Mother Clara's feverish lips, but her tear-bedimmed vision directed toward the crucifix at the foot of the bed was an eloquent *"Fiat!"* to the will of God. Was her work to perish in its initial stage? Could it continue to exist if the Mother were taken away so early from her children?

"Lord—Thy will be done!" breathed her parched lips.

Then Sister Anthony's hand grasped Mother's right hand and pressed it firmly. What was happening to the faithful nurse? Was weakness overcoming her? Pale as death, she sank to her knees at the bedside of her patient. "Yes—if you so will it!" escaped her lips as a sigh; and trembling, she bent over the limp hand of her Mother and kissed it.

Unaccustomed to such behavior, Mother Clara looked up. What was wrong with Sister Anthony? They looked at each other penetratingly; however, they did not fathom the depths of each other's secret: a secret that had arisen between them.

Who would have believed it! Mother Clara recovered. O the joy among her daughters and the children! How many orphans had already feared that they would soon be mother-less for a second time! Now their gratitude knew no end.

When Mother Clara appeared again in the midst of her grown and small children early in May, they surrounded her with great jubilation. Only one was missing. Where was Sister Anthony? She should have led Mother in; it was on her arm that the recuperating Mother had painfully made her first steps.

There was only one shadow on this joyful day—Sister Anthony was sick. As Mother Clara recuperated and became stronger, Sister Anthony felt her first weakness; and as Mother was permitted to rise, Sister Anthony had to take to bed.

Had the care she bestowed on Mother Clara required too much strength? She had never been sick before, and her nature was robust.

Now the roles were exchanged. At Sister Anthony's bed sat Mother Clara. It is true she was not yet able to nurse the sick Sister, but she did not leave the bedside of her dearest daughter. She held her hand soothingly. Whenever Mother's glance sought the crucifix, it implored anxiously: "Lord, leave her with me. By her goodness, mildness, and composure she is a gentle moderator for my willfulness. I need her, Lord. Please let her recover!"

But the Sister's weakness increased daily. Then, in her most serious condition, she was granted her greatest joy—her sick bed was changed into an altar of profession. The end came quickly. With exceptional peace of soul, the young Sister's life slipped away in the arms of Sister Theresa. With her last bit of strength the dying Sister whispered to her with a blissful smile: "For our Mother! Thanks be to God, for he has accepted it!"

Then death closed her lips—a secret had been disclosed.

Deeply moved, Mother Clara made the sign of the cross on the pallid forehead of her daughter. The first victim of death had been demanded of the community. It was a ransom for Mother's life and was paid on May 27, 1861.

Sister Anthony's death proved more painful to Mother Clara than to anyone else. The daughter had been a teacher to the Mother; mildness and patience had been her most precious virtues. The daughter possessed them somewhat naturally; the Mother had to strive daily for them.

Now the triple bond of the founders was likewise broken. Sister Anthony had been a moderator between the two other associates of the foundation. And the Loeser family, which had supported the new community up till now—would it continue to do this?

The number of Sisters grew from month to month, and there was an increase in the number of orphans. The little convent had long since become too small. Surely, a larger house would have to be acquired. But was it judicious to bind themselves to Olpe by purchase? The Bishop had advised them to look about for a new location. The occasional nursing service would remain a sore spot and would give constant cause for conflicts—reason enough for thoughtful consideration of departure. Nevertheless, room would first have to be provided for the growing religious family. What would happen later remained to be seen.

At that time many letters passed from Mother Clara's hands to those of Bishop Conrad Martin, and advice and many proposals came from her exalted protector. The long period of planning closed with a resolute deed—Sister Theresa's mother, Mrs. Bonzel, bought the proposed spacious house with the explanation that it would later be turned over to the Episcopal See. It provided ample room for the Sisters and their charges.

On July 31, 1861, Mother Clara moved into the new home with her family. She was not to feel at home in it very long.

9

The transplanted seedling

HOW MUCH EASIER IT WAS TO ARRANGE AN ORDERLY LIFE in the large house! Mother did not have to fear lack of space for Sisters and children. Scarcely was the turmoil of moving past when she was again able to petition the Bishop for an investiture of nine postulants and, as she modestly added, for the privilege of being herself admitted to final profession, in consideration of her many years as a member of the Community of the Sisters of Christian Charity.

Bishop Conrad Martin most kindly granted both requests and even promised to officiate at the celebration personally. It was a day of great joy, when on August 26, 1861, he visited the community for the first time, gave the holy habit to nine happy children of St. Francis, and accepted the final profession of vows from Mother Clara.

When, in May of the following year, the number of Sisters was again increased by eight novices, Mother Clara was able to open a mission. In October, 1862, she dispatched four Sisters to Much in the Rhineland where they were to be active in education and in the care of the sick.

The young community grew, it is true, in a gratifying way; but the external conflicts did not decrease, and the internal tensions developed imperceptibly. It would indeed be better to look about as soon as possible for a new location.

"Any choice which you make will be satisfactory to me," Bishop Conrad Martin had written a year ago. Mother Clara began to seek for a place in southern Westphalia and in the bishopric of Paderborn.

There was very much to be taken into consideration: Mother Clara preferred above all to live in the vicinity of the episcopal city, in a Catholic territory where no religious Sisters had settled, and in a place located near a railroad. There followed a painstaking search for shelter. Mother Clara's thoughts reverted again and again to the metropolis of the diocese. In Paderborn itself there were already several Mother-houses, but in the surrounding territory there were none.

There was no need to go far beyond Paderborn. On Napoleon's highway, the Hellweg, lay an old city with its salt springs and its wide-spread salt pits—Salzkotten. Yes, this city appeared to be the appropriate spot for an establishment. All the wishes that Mother Clara had concerning the position of the place and the population would be fulfilled in this little country place. A prudent investigation had given her hope. When she traveled with her assistant, Sister Theresa, to Salzkotten on November 15, 1862, she was able to acquire on the east end of the city a larger house with a barn and a garden.

Bishop Conrad Martin had to participate in the joy of this happy solution. In a detailed letter, Mother Clara acquainted him with the purchase of this new property and received an encouraging answer: "I hope that your community will be all the more blessed and will increase by this transfer to Salz-kotten, since I recently learned, during my personal visit there, that everyone is happy about this establishment. As soon as the transfer has taken place, you may come to me; I will then give you useful advice."

In Olpe there was much excitement. Things that were necessary for settling in Salzkotten had to be packed and sent; and a sad time began, especially for the daughters of Olpe They would have a double leave-taking, for the convent in their home town had been dear to them from a two-fold aspect. Many citizens of Olpe, above all the influential relatives of the Sisters, deplored their departure; but they could not order them to stay.

In the beginning of March, 1863, the last arrangements had been made in Salzkotten and in Olpe. Domestic utensils and clothing had been sent from the old home to the new in large shipments. Mother Clara did not wish to give up Olpe entirely. The existing orphanage should become a mission of the Motherhouse. Six Sisters were to remain to care for the children in Olpe. Sister Theresa, who seemed best fitted for the responsibility, would be their Superior.

The days of departure were painful for those who were leaving and for those who remained. Just a few were able to make the distant, expensive journey by coach. Poverty was so great that there was not sufficient traveling fare for all. So most of them prepared to travel on foot.

"A penitential journey," they said. As Mother Clara boarded the tramway with her few companions, her heart ached. How long ago was it when, on this very spot, she alighted from the mail coach and found a hand outstretched to her in loving welcome? Regina Loeser! Mother Clara wept.

The transfer was not possible in one day. In fact, it took some time. The Sisters and postulants traveled in small groups. They also took two orphans with them. These were to form the basic group for the new orphanage at Salzkotten.

On the way, they begged provisions from good people. When, after a fatiguing march, the weary travelers arrived at some locality in the evening, they immediately made a visit to the church and then to the pastor in order to ask for shelter in his parish for the night. By offering hospitality and shelter in their homes, the helpful people sought to alleviate the exertions and difficulties which the day demanded of the travelers.

On the following morning the Sisters met in church and attended Holy Mass. After a substantial breakfast with their hosts, they journeyed on to their first destination, the Pilgrimage Church of Werl, containing the miraculous picture of the Mother of God. Having reached their destination, they took time for a longer rest. What was laid there in devout prayer before the Sorrowful Mother, she had probably never heard before in this old shrine. The pious pilgrims prayed to her for good soil for the transplanted seedling of their community and for favorable weather so that it might grow in its new soil for the honor of God and bring forth fruit. The Sisters also drew her attention to their name: "We are daughters of your Sacred Heart, Mother. You must help us!"

In addition to the food which they begged for the journey, they received occasional small coins along the way from their benevolent benefactors. This provided them with train fare from Werl to Salzkotten. That ride eased their weary limbs.

The Sisters, unaccustomed to traveling on foot, had already gone a distance of ninety kilometers (fifty-six miles). Now their final short train ride brought them quickly to their destination. In Salzkotten Mother Clara awaited them, and the newcomers were made to feel at home.

Thus one group after another arrived at the new Motherhouse. On the feast of St. Joseph, Mother Clara took out of her valise a book in which she had faithfully jotted down the most important events in the life of the community from the very beginning. In large and impressive letters, one striking line stood out amid the many similar notations at the beginning of the chronicle:

Foundation of the Community
October 30, 1860
in Olpe

Under the final brief entry which mentions the packing,
departure, and transfer, Mother Clara drew a heavy line.
Then on a new page she wrote:

Transfer of the Motherhouse from Olpe to Salzkotten
March 19, 1863
with 14 Sisters and 15 Postulants
IN THE NAMES OF JESUS AND MARY!

✠

After years of deep consideration and investigation, the
community had finally found a lasting abode. Mother Clara
was sincerely happy that everything had taken such a peaceful
course. Nevertheless, it was only an apparent peace. Even
though a large group of the citizens of Olpe were in agreement with the transfer of the Motherhouse to Salzkotten, those
families which were close to the Sisters by bonds of relation-
ship and friendship regretted their departure exccedingly.
Moreover, the Sisters themselves who had remained in Olpe
and who for the most part were from southern Westphalia
did not favor the transfer. They preferred to retain as the
Motherhouse the building bought for the community by Sister
Theresa's mother.

The clergy also wanted the central house to be retained at
the place where it had been established. This resulted in
negotiations between Salzkotten and Olpe. With much concern
Mother Clara was opposed to a possible separation and fought
for the maintenance of the orphanage as a mission of the
Salzkotten Motherhouse. The desires of the other side, however, were understandable. The Sisters at Olpe sent a letter

of petition to the Episcopal See asking that their community be recognized as an independent congregation. Bishop Conrad Martin permitted the orphanage at Olpe to be an institution independent of Salzkotten for the time being.

The price of new life is blood and suffering.

Both felt it keenly—Mother Clara and Sister Theresa. When on July 6, 1865, the little community was given episcopal recognition as an independent community under the title "Poor Franciscans of Perpetual Adoration," both of the former associates had to say that God had used them in order to have two blossoms sprout from one bud—both for his honor.

10

Blessed growth and activity

THE MANNER OF LIFE WHICH THE SISTERS HAD BEGUN AND loved in Olpe was faithfully continued in Salzkotten. Immediately after the transfer the Sisters again took as their chief task the adoration of the Blessed Sacrament. Mother Clara's first concern was to transform the barn, belonging to the newly acquired property, into a house of God. This shelter of the Eucharistic Lord became the core of the young community. Certainly great poverty still reigned in the little sanctuary, but in this poverty, so akin to that of the Stable of Bethlehem, Mother Clara spurred her daughters on to intone joyful songs of praise to God.

In the refectory, Holy Poverty, the bride of the Seraphic Father of the Order, was a habitual guest. This, however, did not lessen the joy and the contentment of the children of St. Francis. Most of the time Mother Clara was able to have three meals prepared for her daughters; but the little that graced the table was poorer than alms given to beggars. For breakfast the Sisters always had dried bread with black coffee. Only on Sundays were some turnip tops added to the meal. The sparse midday meal lacked fats; and on weekdays, also meat. Thin soup with dry bread constituted their evening meal.

It continued thus day after day. Moreover, there were also days on which the little bell indeed called the Sisters to table; but the refectorian, who ordinarily served her Sisters like a busy Martha, stood in line with the Sisters and sat down with them to a table that had no food. Mother Clara led the table prayers and gave the signal for spiritual reading. All sat with folded hands and listened to the reading from Holy Scripture. When she tapped the bell to end the reading, Mother Clara stood up and said: "Our dear Lord has fed us today with spiritual nourishment. We wish to thank him for it, and in accordance with the example of our holy Father, St. Francis, let us ask for the true pentitential and religious spirit."

After this the Sisters said their prayer of thanks with contentment and left the refectory hungry.

Their life in the new home spontaneously produced a gradual adjustment into definite religious customs, usages, and stabilization of religious discipline. Whenever the Foundress prayed for a genuine penitential and religious spirit with her daughters, it was no empty formula for her. She vied with them in bearing, in a spirit of Franciscan renunciation and frugality, the poverty forced upon them by circumstances. In a preliminary sketch of the statutes she had devoted special attention to this chapter. Thus one rescript reads:

> Neither the cells nor the beds, nor even medals, crosses, rosaries, books, pictures should be retained by the same Sisters, but the Superior should see that these things are interchanged as often as she considers it judicious.

Mother Clara carried on frequent correspondence with Bishop Conrad Martin during the year of probation. His counsel guided her in revising the religious statutes. She was inclined by nature to severity and to works of self-denial. When she had been seeking permission from the Bishop for the founding of her community, she wrote of her vocation to "a stricter life." As her advisor, the Bishop now had to caution her with fatherly concern while she was formulating the statutes: "I am warning against too great exterior mortification; interior mortification of the will is more important, as I have so often told you."

The Bishop's wise counsel had reference to her associates and her followers. Even though the Foundress loved a hard way of life, this way would not prove feasible for all her daughters. Delicate health and works of charity would not warrant all the Sisters to lead an austere life.

Although she heeded his words of warning, Mother Clara specifically retained severe prescripts relative to fasting in the chapter on "Mortification." More than a third of the year was set aside for fasting. Each evening, with the exception of Easter week, the Sisters retired to their cells where they took the discipline while praying the *Miserere*.

The spirit of penance was a consequence of her deep spirit of prayer. The Constitutions adjoined:

> No matter where the Sisters might be, they should be mindful of the fact that prayer is their chief duty.

"Prayer for the oppressed holy Church" was the most important objective of the community. All prayers of the Sisters were performed with this in mind, especially the prayers said in common.

Mother Francisca Schervier gave the first impetus to pray the Office of the Mother of God when she presented the Marian Office to each of the three young ladies who had sought her advice, as they were leaving Aix-la-Chapelle. Mother Clara had instituted this holy service with her daughters from the very beginning, for she took this seriously. Originally, the community was divided into choir and domestic Sisters; only the former recited the Office. The domestic Sisters prayed a number of *Our Fathers* instead. From 1865 on, the members of the community formed one class only; hence, all were obliged to pray the Marian Office.

Mother Clara herself instructed her daughters in the psalmody, and she insisted that the Latin text be chanted correctly and harmoniously. Woeful lowering of the pitch in the chant of the Office was unbearable to her. Inflexible in her determination that every psalm be started on an elevated tone, she admonished: "Our prayer to God should not be chanted as a lamentation but rather as the song of a soul exulting in the love of God as it unites with the song of the angels."

Is it then surprising that Mother Clara gave the Office priority as the prayer of petition for the Church? To pray for the Church with the words of the Church filled her with heartfelt joy. Completely permeated with the sublimity of this service, she concluded the chapter of the Constitutions on choir prayer in the following manner:

> The Divine Office is an echo of that heavenly harmony in which the angels and saints constantly sing the praise of God. Hence, the Psalmist says: "Blessed are they, O Lord, who dwell in your house; they shall praise you for ever and ever." For in accordance with his promise, our Lord truly deigns to be with us both sacramentally and spiritually. Therefore, it is fitting that we give him praise and honor according to our ability and in conformity with the example of the Church Triumphant. Even though we do not sing his praises unceasingly as the heavenly singers do; at least we appear before him at stated times to render joyful songs of praise.
>
> On high the multitudes sing: "Honor and praise to the Lord"; on earth men following their example unite in the same songs of praise in the chants of the Church. In heaven the Seraphim cry: "Holy, Holy, Holy"; on earth the assembled congregation pours forth the same praise. Thus, heaven and earth unite in a festive celebration.
>
> It is a prayer of thanks, a prayer of praise, a chorus of general rejoicing that the inexpressible goodness of the Lord, who deigned to come down to us, ordained—a chorus that the Holy Ghost assembled. Upon its harmony rests the good

pleasure of the Father. Its melody is from heaven in that it is plucked by the Most Holy Trinity as by a plectrum and reverberates those sweet and blessed melodies, those songs of the angels, those songs of praise which never come to an end.

The solemn observance of the Divine service was a duty ever close to Mother Clara's heart. She had the Sisters participate weekly in an hour of singing under a capable directress so that the singing at Holy Mass and devotions would be truly worthy.

Her spirit of prayer moved her likewise to request a series of prayer-privileges from the Episcopal See for the community. Thus, she asked permission to have hours of reparation on New Year's night, on fast-days, and on the feast of the Sacred Heart. The midnight hour from Thursday to Friday Mother Clara always spent with her daughters before the Tabernacle in remembrance of the sufferings of our Lord in the Garden of Olives.

On the foundation pillars of poverty, of a penitential and religious spirit, and of zealous prayer the Foundress had erected the structure of her home. She was ever alert lest these supports weaken. In conformity to the statutes a Superior had two vigilant Sisters assist her. These were to watch above all for infractions of the rule and, in a spirit of love, to indicate the fault to the erring. Zeal in the observance of the rules prevailed. In order that discipline would not weaken, the Sisters, one by one, knelt every evening before the crucifix in the oratory, to confess before God and their fellow Sisters their failings against the prescripts of the community. This accusation was an incentive to greater fidelity to the rule.

Such pious strivings of the religious family could not fail to bring down blessings. Young girls soon knocked at the convent door and begged admittance. In the fall of the same year of the transfer, the first investiture in Salzkotten took place. Fifteen postulants had come along from Olpe. Since the poorly furnished Motherhouse chapel was too small for the ceremonies, the investiture took place in the time-honored parish church. The people participated joyfully. Thereafter, investitures occurred twice a year for the new members who joined their ranks. Mother Clara manifested the harmony that existed between the community and its Episcopal Protector by setting the date for the fall investiture on the nameday of the Bishop, in order to give him as a nameday gift another group of devotees for holy Church and especially for his bishopric. Bishop Conrad Martin was so happy about this childlike gesture of gratitude that he often personally officiated at the investiture on November 26. It certainly pleased him when a novice received the name of St. Conrad as a title. These thoughtful remembrances served the purpose of affirming the bond of prayer which the community had made with its shepherd.

On the whole, Mother Clara loved to emphasize that they were all mutually "Daughters of the Sacred Hearts of Jesus and Mary" by the title added to the name of each Sister.

She herself, the Foundress of the religious family, alone bore the ecclesiastical foundation title of the community of the Sacred Hearts of Jesus and Mary. However, she reminded her daughters of the veneration of a special mystery of one of these Sacred Hearts by the granting of a title.

She dedicated them to the Heart of Jesus as:

Sister Mary N.
     of the Nativity of Jesus
     of the Poverty of Jesus
     of the Humility of Jesus
     of the Meekness of Jesus
     of the Bitter Passion
     of Christ Crowned with Thorns
     of Christ Carrying the Cross
     of the Five Wounds

of the Wound in Christ's Side
of the Precious Blood
of the Redeemer of the World
of the Most Blessed Sacrament
To the Heart of Mary they were dedicated as:
Sister Mary N.
of the Immaculate Conception
of the Annunciation of Mary
of the Visitation of Mary
of the Seven Joys of Mary
of the Seven Sorrows of Mary
of the Sorrowful Mother
of the Presentation of Mary
of the Assumption of Mary
of the Mother of Mercy
of the Mother of Perpetual Help
of the Queen of the Most Holy Rosary
of the Mother of Victory

This special title attached to their name and given to the Sisters on the day of their investiture was to serve them for their entire religious life as a symbol of exemplary strength. It was to transform them from a child of the world into a true daughter of the Most Sacred Hearts.

The number of Sisters grew rapidly. Thus, Mother Clara was able to give her daughters the same activity as in Olpe. In conjunction with the adoration of the Most Blessed Sacrament and the exercises of piety, they devoted themselves to the education of orphans and the care of the sick—at first only in their homes. The inhabitants of the Salt City and the neighboring villages considered themselves fortunate to be able to entrust their sick to the care of the Sisters. Mother Clara was none the less happy that no boundaries were placed limiting their works of charity.

She soon opened a small preparatory school in order to
be able to give the young girls who had asked for admission
as candidates the preliminary formation leading to the teaching profession. Occasionally, the Sisters also attended these
courses.

The first daughter-houses had already been established
when the Prussian-Austrian war broke out in 1866. Then the
young community had ample opportunities for marks of
Christian charity. Bishop Conrad Martin desired that the
Sisters of his diocese place themselves in the service of the
fatherland. That was as much as a command for Mother Clara.
She assigned fifteen Sisters to care for the wounded and did
not hesitate a moment to go along herself. She appointed a
capable Sister as her substitute and then traveled with her
daughters to the battlefield in Bohemia in order to take charge
of the nursing service in the city and in the castle of Horsitz.
Queen Augusta of Prussia later expressed her thanks in a
grateful decree of praise for the Sisters' wholehearted coopera-
tion in the works of mercy.

They had scarcely returned from the military hospital
service when their country desired their help at home. As a
terrible aftermath of the war, epidemics broke out. Typhus
and cholera claimed their victims. Urgent pleas for help
reached Mother Clara. Despite the small number of Sisters,
she sent nurses everywhere that priests and doctors asked for
them. These deeds of charity afforded the Salzkotten Sisters
wide recognition and in many places of Westphalia, Rhineland, Hannover, and Saxony the foundation stone was laid
for subsequent daughter-houses. The Foundress of the community, however, looked upon this call to charity as a new
indication on the part of God to adopt, along with the education of youth, likewise the care of the sick in their homes
and in hospitals.

The terrors of the pestilence had not yet been entirely dispelled when the hand of God again scourged the country.

1870 to 1871 brought war again, this time Germany against France. And again the fatherland called for nurses. This time Mother Clara freed more than sixty Sisters for first-aid care. When men were again plagued by smallpox, dysentery, and cholera during this war, the Sisters knew what they would have to endure. Not all returned home—the service of obedience at the bedside of the sick took the lives of two young Sisters at the same time. Others returned to the Motherhouse victims of contagious diseases from which they recovered slowly. Mother Clara nursed them herself with self-sacrificing love.

War and epidemics had filled the orphanage at Salzkotten. So the task of providing food and lodging lay as a heavy burden on the heart of Mother Clara. The kindhearted people, above all the noble families of the vicinity, provided the Sisters, who knocked at their doors for provisions, with many gifts. Yet as Mother Clara emptied the baskets, she thought: "What is that for so many?" In order that the children might not starve, Sisters and postulants often had to suffer a great want. Mother suffered hunger with each and every one of them. Moreover, a tremendous burden of work lay on her shoulders: she was simultaneously Mother General and local Superior, she guided the postulancy and the novitiate, and she gave instructions in her beloved orphanage. Correspondence with spiritual and temporal authorities cost her many an hour daily. It was possible to establish at least one daughter-house annually—often even two and three. To accomplish all this, trips and conferences were necessary. Mother Clara did not shirk any difficulties even though her heart condition warned her not to overburden herself. Unyielding energy, strong trust in God, and courageous assurance led her through all difficulties. These traits of character were specifically manifested when there was a question of winning the approval of the civil government for her orphanage as an educational institution. Then this teacher, skilled in the use of words and in the transaction of legal matters, fought an unyielding correspondence battle with the authorities.

In all her cares, Mother Clara found never-failing help in her Episcopal Sponsor, Bishop Conrad Martin. Reverend Edward Klein, appointed Ecclesiastical Moderator by the Bishop, proved to be a wise counselor, especially in the internal formation and the establishment of the community. The religious formation of the youth in the community was especially close to his heart. In those initial years, it had often been necessary to have postulants and novices nurse the sick in their homes or to collect alms. After the years of battle and famine had been withstood, Reverend Klein insisted that the young Sisters of the community be freed from all external activity, such as home-nursing, and receive daily instructions in religion and scientific subjects. Mother Clara, a born teacher, was in accord with the Reverend Moderator. When Sister M. Ignatia, formerly Elizabeth Soentgerath and Mother's best pupil in the preparatory school, had taken her teacher's examination in 1871, Mother Clara appointed her, an exemplary religious, as Novice Mistress. Now the novitiate was in good hands. Mother Clara, freed from this duty, breathed more easily. This change occurred at the right time, because the new Motherhouse was in the process of construction. Even though the property acquired in 1862 had been enlarged by additions, it was no longer large enough to accommodate all the Sisters and orphans. With the approval of Bishop Conrad Martin, the prudent Mother Clara succeeded in acquiring the meadow and garden land opposite the old Motherhouse as property for the construction of the new one. The cornerstone was laid in 1870. On October 28, 1872, the Bishop consecrated the new Motherhouse chapel and blessed the convent.

The great joy of this festive occasion was marred by the threatening storm that rose over entire Germany—the Kultur-kampf (Falk Laws).

11

In the tempest

FOR A DECADE, SALZKOTTEN HAD BEEN THE HOME OF THIS
Franciscan family, and its members were already active in
22 daughter-houses located in various parts of Germany.
From the beginning of the foundation of the community, the
Sisters were active in schools and hospitals. Then the severe
Kulturkampf laws put all communities in dire distress. At the
beginning of the Kulturkampf, a ministerial order had closed
the elementary schools to religious women. That already had
been a severe blow for Mother Clara's work. It struck her
harder when the law against religious later forbade the Sisters
to take part in any type of educational activity in Prussia.
Along with the care of the sick, the Salzkotten Sisters had
devoted themselves above all to instruction and education in
orphanages and kindergartens, in elementary schools, and in
sewing and domestic schools. The order of the Minister dissolved six of these schools besides some boarding schools and
orphanages. The only task left to the religious women was
care of the sick.

The Motherhouse was filled with teaching Sisters, who had
returned home from educational institutions that had been
closed.

Where should she send them? They could not remain in Salzkotten; there was not enough work and food for so many. Hence, it was imperative to seek new fields of endeavor. Mother Clara was compelled to make contacts abroad.

Before the outbreak of the Kulturkampf some Sisters had been sent to Metz. Nursing of the sick and wounded during the German-Franco war had made the Franciscans from Salzkotten popular in that place. As a consequence, immediately after the war Mother Clara was asked to take over the St. Blandina Institute for girls in Metz. She gladly acceded to this request. In conjunction with this home for girls she simultaneously established a private German elementary school. When the Jesuit College of the city was dissolved in 1872, the Sisters opened a hospital in this spacious building. Thus Mother, so burdened with care, had the opportunity of providing a place for a number of the Sisters who were without work in their native country. There in Alsace-Lorraine they might continue the work of education, instruction, and nursing.

The first seed had been planted for a later independent province abroad.

North America also called for Sisters. In a pleading letter, the pastor of St. Boniface Church in Carondelet, near St. Louis, Missouri, had applied to the Episcopal See of Paderborn for German Sisters to undertake the management of a hospital. Bishop Conrad Martin thought immediately of "his community." He did not approach Mother Clara in vain. Without delay, she placed the Bishop's request before her daughters. She did not have to beg for volunteers for this difficult task because a large group declared itself ready. Mother selected three experienced nurses, who set sail in December, 1872. Soon there followed a second and a third group, each consisting of eight Sisters. A foreign land called for the service of charity; their own native country no longer wanted their service. Under such circumstances, Mother sadly let her daughters go. The uncertain lot of those remaining behind made the separation doubly difficult for the departing Sisters, whose cheerful, self-sacrificing obedience became a source of blessing to the second planting abroad.

The pressure of the Kulturkampf forced Mother Clara not only to seek work for her daughters abroad but also to depend upon the charity of strangers for the sustenance of those entrusted to her care. With the approval of the respective Bishops, she sent Sisters to nearby Holland. The collection tours were not easy for those who were sent. However, the Dutch people not only showed themselves sympathetic but even glad to give alms, and the Sisters had many opportunities to experience the truth of the "proverbial friendliness" of the Dutch. Through these collection tours, contact was established with Holland. When, therefore, the Sisters again showed up in Holland in 1875 to start a new field of activity, they met with immediate success and thereby planted the third seed abroad. They were able to devote themselves unhindered to the tasks of education and care of the sick. Mother Clara erected a number of small daughter-houses and thus created the basic foundation for the later Holland Province of the community.

The number of houses abroad grew from year to year, and Mother's concern about her work grew constantly. The administration of all these missions was still dependent upon the Motherhouse. Determination and trust in God had helped the Foundress in the time of oppression to venture one daughter-house after the other. In making such new establishments, her conviction in her own decisions, combined with the wise counsel of her Episcopal Protector, proved advantageous. Now, more than ever, she also knew how to treasure the assistance of the intelligent and circumspect Reverend Klein. Cooperating with him, she managed to bring the flourishing orphanage in Salzkotten through the storms of the Kulturkampf to peaceful times.

12

The burning seal

NOT ONE HOUR, SINCE THE FOUNDATION OF THE COMMUNITY, did the daughters of St. Francis cease to pray for the oppressed holy Church. More fervently than ever did the Sisters now pray for the flock of Christ and its shepherds. With anxious concern, these faithful souls prayed especially for their beloved Bishop Conrad Martin. At the very beginning of the Kulturkampf he had appeared at the scene of battle as a courageous leader, and from then on he stood in the first rank as a defender of the rights of the Church. Thus, it could not be otherwise than that he become the first victim of the blows of the enemy.

The fearless champion clearly foresaw his imprisonment. Repeatedly he summoned Mother Clara to Paderborn to discuss with her important questions concerning the community. The fate of his Sisters filled him with great concern. As yet, the lawless enactments had not touched the core of religious life. If it should happen that even admission of candidates and the profession of vows should come under the control of the civil government—then, double woe to religious families! All possibilities of such tyranny were seriously considered in these discussions between the Bishop and Mother Clara. They sought ways and means to withstand the enemy.

Finally that occurred which all the faithful of the diocese had feared. The "troublesome admonisher" and intrepid fighter in violet garb was silenced. A wave of revolt ran through the country when it became known that the Prince of the Church was imprisoned. The episcopal city trembled with helpless agitation. On the day of imprisonment a mass of people gathered in the streets leading to the episcopal palace. After a long delay the convicted man, pale but erect, appeared at the entrance of his house. Under guard he was led to the coach that would bring him to prison. It was almost impossible for the coach to start. Shoulder to shoulder, the crowd moved along in the same direction. After a painfully slow trip, the coach finally reached its destination, and the otherwise rugged man climbed wearily up the high steps of the prison. There he beheld the flock of his faithful that looked like a densely packed herd of cattle. He glanced over the crowd sorrowfully. Then he stood erect and raised his hand in a farewell blessing. Weeping, the people remained on their knees as their Father disappeared behind the strong iron door.

That was October 4, 1874. The Episcopal See was empty. When the terrible news reached the Motherhouse at Salzkotten, Mother Clara rang the bell for prayer. The Sisters and their pupils were told what had happened. They left their work and hastened to the chapel which soon resounded with pleading cries to heaven: "We beseech Thee, hear us," as Mother Clara led the litany of all Saints.

That thou wouldst vouchsafe to govern and preserve thy holy Church . . .

That thou wouldst vouchsafe to preserve our Apostolic Prelate and all Orders of the Church in holy religion . . .

That thou wouldst vouchsafe to humble the enemies of holy Church . . .

That thou wouldst vouchsafe to give peace and unity to all Christian people . . .

Just as Mother Clara had been a frequent guest in the episcopal residence during the anxious weeks before the imprisonment so now she was a faithful visitor at the prison as often as she could obtain permission to enter. The supervisor of the prison was more human than he who, by his authority in the government, had confined the Bishop to prison. The kind supervisor recognized the friends of the Bishop and was less attentive when, at twilight, they came either to bring consolation to the prisoner or to seek his advice.

Yes, advice! The Bishop did not bury himself in self-pity and depression. His body alone lived within four bare, cold walls; his thoughts and concern were outside with his flock. Before Mother Clara could inquire about his health while visiting him, the Bishop had already asked about the welfare of his daughters who, behind the convent walls, were endeavoring to check the storm by their prayers.

The Bishop saw it clearly: if the elements inimical to God were given complete reign, then all was over with Catholic religious life, all was over with his beloved community; and, if the intrigue of the enemy would kill him, then Mother Clara would be abandoned and without counsel. He had to give her full power so that she might independently take care of matters in the hour of still greater need and in order that the continued existence of the community might be insured.

For a long time the Bishop pondered; then in prayer it became clear to him how he was to help the Superior of the community.

She came again to bring him the consolation that his Sisters were praying unceasingly for him. The prisoner kindly thanked her for this gift of love. Then he pushed a document to her through the grating. With a questioning glance, Mother Clara accepted it.

With that, they heard the guard approaching. The right hand of the Bishop, wearing the ring of God-given-power and dignity, was raised in blessing. She knelt down and concealed the letter under her scapular beneath the emblem of the pierced hearts. A hot, sickening feeling took hold of her. The document rested on her breast like a burning seal.

The Bishop had just enough time to say: "I command you in obedience to the Church to absolute silence toward everyone. The document contains secret plenary powers concerning which no one may know—not even the Ecclesiastical Moderator—so that he may be secure against eventual plots on the part of the government."

At this command, the startled Sister felt as though the seal burned more intensely. It lay upon her like a sentence of death, and yet the commission had been given to her so that her daughters might live.

In the solitude of her cell Mother Clara read the few lines. It is appalling what she was commissioned to do. She was given secret plenary power:

> To accept and invest postulants,
> To administer the property of the community,
> To accept and discontinue daughter-houses.

Each line indicated his concern about the constancy and the growth of the community; concern also, however, about the Reverend Moderator, lest he receive the same treatment as his Bishop. Therefore, the Reverend Moderator must not know about the privileges so that he might freely state before the court that he had no part in them.

Several years had passed since Mother Clara held a similar important document in her trembling hands—an approval to found her community. The present document dealt with preserving its continued existence. At that time she was permitted to show that first document to her co-founders with grateful joy; now she would have to conceal this secret document from everyone.

Writing-room, cell, and archives of the cloister were too insecure against the house-searchings of the enemies of religion. There remained no more secret place for the document than the heart of the Mother.

There it lay well-preserved in a leathern pouch; her lips were silent.

When would she have to act for the first time in accordance with these plenary powers? Her soul was filled with divided sentiments since her last visit to the prison. She was proud and happy in the confidence which her Bishop had shown her, but this happiness was subdued by the tormenting fear: how will the Reverend Moderator, the spiritual authorities, and, last but not least, her own daughters accept it when, with complete independence, she would carry out functions that were not hers by universal law and custom?

The time had not yet come to have recourse to the secret plenary powers. Perhaps, the hour would never come. May God so dispose! How gladly she would then give back the sublime commission into the hands of the Bishop.

But the battle raged on.

In the days of anxiety about the fate of the Bishop, the joyful news brought the consolation that he had been liberated from prison after he had finished his term. However, this joy was soon marred by new apprehensions. The intrigues of the government against this indomitable champion of rights did not lessen. In January, 1875, the government passed a sentence which deprived him of all episcopal rights and functions and sentenced him again to nine months' imprisonment in the fortress of Wesel. Before the sentence ran its course, he made his escape; after months of wandering about and of being pursued by the Prussian regime, he found secure refuge in Belgium.

Mother Clara stood all alone with her cares and her secret. She had to take more and more Sisters out of educational activities and give them other tasks at home and abroad. The number of members had increased considerably.

On December 2, 1875, Mother Clara again gave her farewell blessing to five brave daughters for their journey over the ocean. They were to board the steamer "Deutschland" on December 5 at the port in Bremen. Among the Sisters was one who according to the plan of the Foundress would guide the American Province with wise circumspection. For it became more and more evident that it was too difficult to guide the daughter-houses in America from Salzkotten. Therefore, Mother Clara fostered the plan of uniting these American houses into an independent province. With watchful eye, she tested her daughters for a period of time to discern the one, whom she might one day appoint as Provincial Superior.

Her choice fell upon Sister Henrica Fassbender. Intelligence, prudence, motherliness, and piety were the excellent qualifications which Sister Henrica possessed. Indeed, the commission was hard for both Mother and daughter. They were truly devoted to each other. Mother Clara lost in Sister Henrica a promising source of strength for work in the fatherland, but the welfare of the community surpassed all personal considerations and desires on the part of the Superior General.

The departure was hard for the five young Sisters who went in virtue of obedience. Early on the day of departure, four of them pronounced their perpetual vows; and one, her temporary vows. With eagerness, they generously accepted their commission.

Again and again they recommended themselves to the prayers of those remaining at home. The Sisters at the

Motherhouse immediately began to keep hours of adoration before the Blessed Sacrament to plead for a safe journey for the travelers. They intended to do this until word of their safe arrival had come from America.

When, with a heavy heart, Mother Clara returned to her cell after their departure, she found a letter lying on her desk. It bore Sister Henrica's handwriting.

She opened it and read:

FAREWELL

Now the solemn hour of departure is at hand,
And my heart, deeply touched, throbs with fear;
'Tis bleeding as though pierced by many a spear,
For in bitter pain we leave you and our land so dear.

I leave—yes, depart gladly and in peace—
In obedience to your wishes, O Mother most dear;
Though distant, I know that your prayers will ne'er cease,
For your love will follow—hov'ring ever near.

Yet, poor nature doth press its human rights so—
Clinging in anguish to you and the fatherland blest;
Thus, from a torn heart, these hot tears do flow
Mingled with many a sigh from my burdened breast.

But oh! as once again before you I kneel,
Allow these tears of departure free reign—
Thus consoled, I shall depart; for I shall feel
Your precious blessing coming to us o'er the main.

Yes, bless me, Mother! God can and will heed
The prayerful blessing your fingers trace on me;
I need not fear—God knows best my every need—
Is he not ruler over land and sea?

For me beg the courage, the strength, and the power
That holy zeal for his honor within me may burn;
That humbly his glory I increase in each hour,
While striving his Holy Will to perform.

May I never fall into self-complacency vain,
Forgetting the promise and pledge I now raise;
To please God alone, I seek! His Will shall reign—
E'en though my work from others gain praise.

O pray that this office upon me now laid
Shall not too heavy for my weak shoulders prove;
May I learn to bear all with soul unafraid
While for Gods' highest honor, I labor with love.

Now farewell! Receive as a last little cession
My heart with filial gratitude aglow;
In fidelity to obedience, this last possession
Into your hands, my consecrate heart I bestow.

Farewell! Farewell! For I must now depart,
Yet will remain in spirit ever close to you!
Enclosed forever within Jesus' Sacred Heart,
Your joys and sorrows will be mine too!

Farewell! also to you, my Sisters fond—
Ever preserve in your hearts your love for me!
Thus, uniting more firmly the consecrate bond
That binds our hearts for all eternity.

Farewell! Hallowed Spot, where so oft I have knelt
Farewell! Our Convent Chapel, so dear!
For here in thy sanctuary oft have I felt
God's plea: "Draw nigh to me here!"

Farewell! Holy Statues—perhaps forever!
You who so peacefully down upon me gaze,
As though you'd say: "You too must endeavor
Your eyes to Heaven always to raise!"

Farewell! Farewell! You Hallowed Rooms—
Where I have lived so happily without pain;
Farewell; You Gardens and all you lovely trees—
Farewell! Farewell! and Auf Wiedersehn!

Dedicated to our dearly beloved Venerable Mother
at our departure for America
by
Your loving daughter, grateful unto death,
Sister M. Henrica

Salzkotten, December 2, 1875

Of all those who emigrated, no one had said farewell so touchingly. Sister Henrica was only twenty-eight years old. Only in obedience was the sacrifice of separation possible for her. But her profession of vows made her strong. With tear-filled eyes, Mother Clara read repeatedly the last lines of her daughter: "Your loving daughter, grateful unto death."

Then came the tragic news: the ocean voyage had become a death voyage. On the very first day the steamer was dashed to pieces on a sandbank in a foggy storm at the mouth of the Thames. Many passengers drowned; among them the five Sisters.

The news left Mother Clara benumbed with sorrow. It seemed incomprehensible. She remained a long time before the Tabernacle in tears and finally wrung a *Fiat* from her heart. Then with the deeply afflicted Sisters, she prayed the *De Profundis* five times.

When it became known shortly after that in the face of certain death the heroic Salzkotten Franciscans had strengthened their despairing fellow-passengers up to the last moment by stimulating their confidence in God and their resignation to His Holy Will, and that they had even rejected the lifeboats so that fathers, mothers, and children might be saved, the deeply grieved Sisters added a silent *Deo Gratias* that God had deigned to allow their brave Sisters to die a death of love.

THE WRECK OF THE DEUTSCHLAND*

Part the First

1

Thou mastering me
God! giver of breath and bread;
World's strand, sway of the sea;
Lord of living and dead;
Thou hast bound bones and veins in me, fastened me flesh,
And after it almost unmade, what with dread,
Thy doing: and dost thou touch me afresh?
Over again I feel thy finger and find thee.

2

I did say yes
O at lightning and lashed rod;
Thou heardest me truer than tongue confess
Thy terror, O Christ, O God;
Thou knowest the walls, altar and hour and night:
The swoon of a heart that the sweep and the hurl of thee trod
Hard down with a horror of height:
And the midriff astrain with leaning of, laced with fire of stress.

3

Tho frown of his face
Before me, the hurtle of hell
Behind, where, where was a, where was a place?
I whirled out wings that spell
And fled with a fling of the heart to the heart of the Host.
My heart, but you were dovewinged, I can tell,
Carrier-witted, I am bold to boast,
To flash from the flame to the flame then, tower from the grace
to the grace.

---

*This poem, taken from *Poems of Gerard Manley Hopkins* S.N., which
is edited by Robert Bridges, depicts the tragic wreck of the "Deutschland" in which the five Franciscans of our community lost their lives.
It has been inserted with the permission of the Oxford University Press,
London.

4

I am soft sift
In an hourglass — at the wall
Fast, but mined with a motion, a drift
And it crowds and it combs to the fall;
I steady as a water in a well, to a poise, to a pane,
But roped with, always, all the way down from the tall
Fells or flanks of the voel, a vein
Of the gospel proffer, a pressure, a principle, Christ's gift.

5

I kiss my hand
To the stars, lovely-asunder
Starlight, wafting him out of it; and
Glow, glory in thunder;
Kiss my hand to the dappled-with-damson west:
Since, tho' he is under the world's splendour and wonder,
His mystery must be instressed, stressed;
For I greet him the days I meet him, and bless when I understand.

6

Not out of his bliss
Springs the stress felt
Nor first from heaven (and few know this)
Swings the stroke dealt —
Stroke and a stress that stars and storms deliver,
That guilt is hushed by, hearts are flushed by and melt —
But it rides time like riding a river
(And here the faithful waver, the faithless fable and miss).

7

It dates from day
Of his going in Galilee;
Warm-laid grave of a womb-life grey;
Manger, maiden's knee;
The dense and the driven Passion, the frightful sweat;
Thence the discharge of it, there its swelling to be,
Though felt before, though in high flood yet —
What none would have known of it, only the heart, being hard
at bay.

8

Is out with it! Oh,
We lash with the best or worst
Word last! How a lush-kept plush-capped sloe
Will, mouthed to flesh-burst,
Gush! — flush the man, the being with it, sour or sweet,
Brim, in a flash, full! — Hither then, last or first,
To hero of Calvary, Christ's feet —
Never ask if meaning it, wanting it, warned of it — men go.

9

Be adored among men,
God, three-numbered form;
Wring thy rebel, dogged in den,
Man's malice, with wrecking and storm.
Beyond saying sweet, past telling of tongue,
Thou art lightning and love, I found it, a winter and warm;
Father and fondler of heart thou hast wrung:
Hast thy dark descending and most art merciful then.

10

With an anvil-ding
And with fire in him forge thy will
Or rather, rather then, stealing as Spring
Through him, melt him but master him still:
Whether at once, as once at a crash Paul
Or as Austin, a lingering-out sweet skill,
Make mercy in all of us, out of us all
Mastery, but be adored, but be adored King.

Part the Second

11

'Some find me a sword; some
The flange and the rail; flame,
Fang, or flood' goes Death on drum,
And storms bugle his fame.
But we dream, we are rooted in earth — Dust!
Flesh falls within sight of us, we, though our flower the same,
Wave with the meadow, forget that there must
The sour scythe cringe, and the blear share come.

12

On Saturday sailed from Bremen,
American-outward-bound.
Take settler and seamen, tell men with women,
Two hundred souls in the round —
O Father, not under thy feathers nor even as guessing
The goal was a shoal, of a fourth the doom to be drowned;
Yet did the dark side of the bay of they blessing
Not vault them, the millions of rounds of thy mercy not reeve
even them in?

13

Into the snows she sweeps,
Hurling the haven behind,
The Deutschland, on Sunday; and so the sky keeps,
For the infinite air is unkind,
And the sea flint-flake, black-backed in the regular blow,
Sitting Eastnortheast, in cursed quarter, the wind;
Wiry and white-fiery and whirlwind-swivelled snow
Spins to the widow-making unchilding unfathering deeps.

14

She drove in the dark to leeward,
She struck — not a reef or a rock
But the combs of a smother of sand; night drew her
Dead to the Kentish Knock;
And she beat the bank down with her bows and the ride of
her keel:
The breakers rolled on her beam with ruinous shock;
And canvas and compass, the whorl and the wheel
Idle for ever to waft her or wind her with, these she endured.

15

Hope had grown grey hairs,
Hope had mourning on,
Trenched with tears, carved with cares,
Hope was twelve hours gone;
And frightful a nightfall folded rueful a day
Nor rescue, only rocket and lightship, shone,
And lives at last were washing away:
To the shrouds they took,—they shook in the hurling and
horrible airs.

16

One stirred from the rigging to save
The wild woman-kind below,
With a rope's end round the man, handy and brave —
He was pitched to his death at a blow,
For all his dreadnought breast and braids of thew:
They could tell him for hours, dandled the to and fro
Through the cobbled foam-fleece, what could he do
With the burl of the fountains of air, buck and the flood of the
wave?

17

They fought with God's cold —
And they could not and fell to the deck
(Crushed them) or water (and drowned them) or rolled
With the sea-romp over the wreck.
Night roared, with the heart-break hearing a heart-broke
rabble
The woman's wailing, the crying of child without check —
Till a lioness arose breasting the babble,
A prophetess towered in the tumult, a virginal tongue told.

18

Ah, touched in your bower of bone
Are you! turned for an exquisite smart,
Have you! make words break from me here all alone,
Do you! — mother of being in me, heart.
O unteachable after evil, but uttering truth,
Why, tears! is it? tears; such a melting, a madrigal start!
Never-eldering revel and river of youth,
What can it be, this glee? the good you have there of your own?

19

Sister, a sister calling
A master, her master and mine! —
And the inboard seas run swirling and hawling;
The rash smart sloggering brine
Blinds her; but she that weather sees one thing, one;
Has one fetch in her: she rears herself to divine
Ears, and the call of the tall nun
To the men in the tops and the tackle rode over the storm's
brawling.

20

She was first of a five and came
Of a coifed sisterhood.
(O Deutschland, double a desperate name!
O world wide of its good!
But Gertrude, lily, and Luther, are two of a town,
Christ's lily and beast of the waste wood:
From life's dawn it is drawn down,
Abel is Cain's brother and breasts they have suckled the same.)

21

Loathed for a love men knew in them,
Banned by the land of their birth,
Rhine refused them. Thames would ruin them;
Surf, snow, river and earth
Gnashed: but thou art above, thou Orion of light;
Thy unchancelling poising palms were weighing the worth,
Thou martyr-master: in thy sight
Storm flakes were scroll-leaved flowers, lily showers—sweet
heaven was astrew in them.

22

Five! the finding and sake
And cipher of suffering Christ.
Mark, the mark is of man's make
And the word of it Sacrificed.
But he scores it in scarlet himself on his own bespoken,
Before-time-taken, dearest prized and priced—
Stigma, signal, cinquefoil token
For lettering of the lamb's fleece, ruddying of the rose-flake.

23

Joy fall to thee, father Francis,
Drawn to the Life that died;
With the gnarls of the nails in thee, niche of the lance, his
Lovescape crucified
And seal of his seraph-arrival! and these thy daughters
And five-lived and leaved favour and pride,
Are sisterly sealed in wild waters,
To bathe in his fall-gold mercies, to breathe in his all-fire glances.

24

Away in the loveable west,
On a pastoral forehead of Wales,
I was under a roof here, I was at rest,
And they the prey of the gales;
She to the black-about air, to the breaker, the thickly
Falling flakes, to the throng that catches and quails
Was calling 'O Christ, Christ, come quickly':
The cross to her she calls Christ to her, christens her wild-worst
Best.

25

The majesty! what did she mean?
Breathe, arch and original Breath.
Is it love in her of the being as her lover had been?
Breathe, body of lovely Death.
They were else-minded then, altogether, the men
Woke thee with a *we are perishing* in the weather of
Gennesareth.
Or is it that she cried for the crown then,
The keener to come at the comfort for feeling the combating keen?

26

For how to the heart's cheering
The down-dugged ground-hugged grey.
Hovers off, the jay-blue heaven appearing
Of pied and peeled May!
Blue-beating and hoary-glow height; or night, still higher,
With belled fire and the moth-soft Milky Way,
What by your measure is the heaven of desire,
The treasure never eyesight got, nor was ever guessed what for
the hearing?

27

No, but it was not these.
The jading and jar of the cart,
Time's tasking, it is fathers that asking for ease
Of the sodden-with-its-sorrowing heart,
Not danger, electrical horror; then further it finds
The appealing of the Passion is tenderer in prayer apart:
Other, I gather, in measure her mind's
Burden, in wind's burly and beat of endragoned seas.

28

But how shall I . . . make me room there:
Reach me a . . . Fancy, come faster —
Strike you the sight of it? look at it loom there,
Thing that she . . . there then! the Master,
Ipse, the only one, Christ, King, Head:
He was to cure the extremity where he had cast her;
Do, deal, lord it with living and dead;
Let him ride, her pride, in his trumph, despatch and have done
with his doom there.

29

Ah! there was a heart right!
There was single eye!
Read the unshapeable shock night
And knew the who and the why;
Wording it how but by him that present and past,
Heaven and earth are word of, worded by? —
The Simon Peter of a soul! to the blast
Tarpeian-fast, but a blown beacon of light.

30

Jesu, heart's light,
Jesu, maid's son,
What was the feast followed the night
Thou hadst glory of this nun? —
Feast of the one woman without stain,
For so conceived, so to conceive thee is done;
But here was heart-throe, birth of a brain,
Word, that heard and kept thee and uttered thee outright.

31

Well, she has thee for the pain, for the
Patience; but pity of the rest of them!
Heart, go and bleed at a bitterer vein for the
Comfortless unconfessed of them —
No not uncomforted: lovely-felicitous Providence
Finger of a tender of, O of a feathery delicacy, the breast of the
Maiden could obey so, be a bell to, ring of it, and
Startle the poor sheep back! is the shipwreck then a harvest,
does tempest carry the grain for thee?

32

I admire thee, master of the tides,
  Of the Yore-flood, of the year's fall;
The recurb and the recovery of the gulf's sides,
  The girth of it and the wharf of it and the wall;
Stanching, quenching ocean of a motionable mind;
  Ground of being, and granite of it: past all
    Grasp God, throned behind
Death with a sovereignty that heeds but hides, bodes but abides:

33

With a mercy that outrides
  The all of water, an ark
For the listener; for the lingerer with a love glides
  Lower than death and the dark;
A vein for the visiting of the past-prayer, pent in prison.
  The-last-breath penitent spirits — the uttermost mark
    Our passion-plunged giant risen,
The Christ of the Father compassionate, fetched in the storm of
    his strides.

34

Now burn, new born to the world,
  Double-natured name,
The heaven-flung, heart-fleshed, maiden-furled
  Miracle-in-Mary-of-flame,
Mid-numbered He in three of the thunder-throne!
  Not a dooms-day dazzle in his coming nor dark as he came;
    Kind, but royally reclaiming his own;
A released shower, let flash to the shire, not a lightning of fire
    hard-hurled.

35

Dame, at our door
  Drowned, and among our shoals,
Remember us in the roads, the heaven-haven of the Reward:
  Our King back, oh, upon English souls!
Let him easter in us, be a dayspring to the dimness of us, be
    a crimson-cresseted east,
  More brightening her, rare-dear Britain, as his reign rolls,
    Pride, rose, prince, hero of us, high-priest.
Our hearts' charity's heart's fire, our thoughts' chivalry's throng's
    Lord.

Oppression on the part of the government became increasingly difficult. Up till now the laws of the Kulturkampf had crippled the activity of the religious women in schools and homes. Now it dug into the very core of conventual life. A governmental decree of May, 1875, ruled that, in the educational institutions still existing, no change would be permitted in the number of Sisters and that ministerial permission must be obtained for the reception of new members into the community.

This decree was a direct blow at the very roots of religious life.

Between 1875 and 1876, over sixty postulants waited for an investiture. According to the law against religious, permission for the investiture had to be obtained from the Minister of Education and the Minister of the Interior. A consequence of this decree would be—at least externally—a recognition of the law. And who could tell whether the answer might not be negative. At the very least, one had to reckon with the control over the placements of the respective Sisters in the daughter-houses.

All had developed as the exiled Bishop had foreseen with great anxiety. Mother Clara felt that the time had come to be mindful of the secret plenary powers.

The secret lying on her heart seemed to burn more intensely.

Thirteen novices had finished their year of probation on July 1, 1875, and were looking forward to their first profession. There was nothing in the state laws that forbade the profession of religious vows, and yet the anxious Superior General proceeded cautiously. The day and the hour were kept secret. No one was invited to the celebration—even the employees of the convent knew nothing. Behind locked doors of the Motherhouse chapel, Reverend Moderator Klein accepted the temporary profession of the novices. Mother Clara saw her wise measures of precaution rewarded; no spy had disrupted the ceremony. So much the greater was their alarm however, when the Reverend Moderator was suddenly summoned to court in Paderborn. A complaint had been filed against him with the district attorney by some unknown person that by the acceptance of vows he had arrogated to himself episcopal rights; in addition, because of his part in this ceremony, he was accused of failing against the law affecting religious. At the trial, the fearless and clever defendant pleaded that a profession of vows does not increase the number of Sisters in the community and that the increase takes place only by investiture. And had he arrogated episcopal rights? The ceremony of investiture and profession were exactly the special obligations of a Moderator.

To the chagrin of the district attorney, the Reverend Moderator Klein was acquitted.

Mother Clara's anxiety, however, grew; for the authorities were on the alert and the Motherhouse was under constant surveillance. What was she to do with the postulants who wished to receive the habit? With a heavy heart she decided to send a number of the candidates home again with the assurance that they would be called back later. But she could not do that with all of them. The daughter-houses—above all, those abroad—wanted more help. What was she to do? She dared not and would not go to the state authority. There was only one thing to do—invest secretly. But alas, if that too should become known! A simple royal decree would have been able to suppress the Motherhouse. The preparation for the planned investiture on May 28, 1876, had to be made still more secretly than that for the profession. This time it would again be a ceremony within a restricted group of Sisters. No outsider knew anything about it. Early on the day of the investiture six postulants, in white bridal dress and long veil knelt in the oratory of the Motherhouse. Mother Clara and the Novice Mistress, Sister Ignatia, prayed with them. Reverend Moderator Klein wanted to invest the postulants. How long he kept them waiting! Had he perhaps fallen into the hands of the police? Hours passed. Noon came—still he had not arrived. Those to be invested grew tense, and the concern of Mother Clara increased. Finally, she said: "Put aside the bridal dress and preserve your heart in peace. The hour of the Bridegroom has not yet come."

Perhaps unforeseen official duties had detained the Reverend Moderator in the morning. He would very probably come in the afternoon. Therefore, the six postulants prepared and again waited in their white bridal attire hour after hour. In the evening Mother Clara announced: "We will pray *Compline* and go to rest; it seems that the Lord has not found us ready enough today."

Then, in the early hours of the night the Novice Mistress wrapped on the cell doors of the postulants: "The Bridegroom is here. Rise! Go to meet him."

Completely alert after their short slumber, the brides put on their festive garb for the third time; and, in the secret stillness, the holy event took place in the oratory by candlelight. Apart from the Reverend Moderator, who had stolen like a thief in the night to the Motherhouse, only Mother Clara and the Mistress were present. They spent the night in prayer with the happy novices. A holy night it was; for, at dawn, the young daughters of St. Francis experienced the second great act of their religious life. In consideration of the extraordinary circumstances of the Kulturkampf, Moderator Klein with full episcopal powers had declared that the newly invested might immediately make their temporary profession of vows. In the early morning hours they were admitted in all secrecy to temporary profession during a low Mass in the oratory. Scarcely had an hour passed after this ceremony, so similar to that of the catacombs, when the newly professed were on their way to Paderborn in the convent coach. There they were to take the early express train to Metz. Mother Clara did not breathe freely until news of the happy arrival came a few days later from the distant imperial territory of Alsace-Lorraine, where the Prussian law against religious was not effective. Thanks be to God! And she acquired courage for more secret investitures.

13

The tragedy of sealed lips

A WHOLE YEAR PASSED BY WITHOUT THE MOTHER GENERAL
being able to satisfy the pleading requests of daughter-houses
for more Sisters in Metz and Holland. Indeed, nine postulants
were again waiting to receive the habit, but the times were too
dangerous. Reverend Moderator Klein was not able to give
them the holy garb because spies lurked at every door of the
Motherhouse.

More than ever, Mother Clara joined the Sisters in adoration. As she knelt before the Tabernacle, she often unfolded
her hands and placed them either protectingly or imploringly
over her heart. Should she now carry out the episcopal mandate which the Bishop had given her? Did she not have to
do it now?

The longer she weighed this question in prayer, the clearer
it became to her: "Yes, she was authorized to, and she had
to." And this certainty led her immediately to conceive a plan:
On June 1, 1877, the nine waiting postulants will receive the
habit of the Order by my hands.

Upon this resolve, hot blood rushed through her veins; the
burning seal suddenly stabbed her heart painfully. She foresaw
it now with certainty that the great passion-time of her life
was now beginning.

All external preparations for the investiture were once more made in secret. Only a few Sisters knew about it. During a quiet week of contemplation, Mother Clara and the Mistress of Novices had helped the nine postulants by lectures and conferences to prepare themselves interiorly for the great day.

A firm bond of mutual trust existed between Mother Clara and her most loyal daughter, Sister Ignatia. The Foundress had never regretted entrusting the youth of the community to this conscientious Sister. They were always in perfect agreement on all religious questions.

On the eve of the investiture, she summoned the Novice Mistress and the sacristan and told the latter: "Tomorrow, you need not set out priestly vestments for the ceremony." Both Sisters believed that the investiture had been postponed. Astonished, they wanted to ask why. Mother Clara looked into their startled faces and answered merely: "I, myself, will invest them."

What Mother was saying could not be true. Such an act was unprecedented. Never before had postulants received their holy garb from unconsecrated hands. Had Mother forgotten that the right of investiture belonged only to the Bishop or to one delegated by him? And such a commission was given only to a priest. Granted that the Bishop was in exile and that the Reverend Moderator could not be reached. But could not the convent chaplain perform the investiture? How could Mother assume such rights?

The disconcerted look of both Sisters spoke more eloquently than words. It reflected unbelieving horror, contradiction, and even rebellion. When the sacristan left the room after a painful silence, Mother Clara and Sister Ignatia remained alone.

Then the conscientious Novice Mistress remonstrated, pleaded, entreated with her not to encroach on the rights of the holy priesthood, for that would bring ruin and not blessing. One must at least wait, if no priest can perform the ceremony.

Was that still the modest, reserved, obedient Sister Ignatia? Never had Mother Clara heard such speech from her. When had she ever dared to contradict Mother General? Now she was saying with earnest mien and in a decisive tone: "That will not work, Reverend Mother! You are not allowed to act thus!"

These two, who until now had been one in all things, stood facing each other. When, instead of vindicating or explaining, Mother Clara quietly repeated: "I, myself, will invest them!" Sister Ignatia knew that all contradictions were to no purpose, and she left in tears.

Motionless, Mother watched her depart. Then her hands opened and closed convulsively on her breast! "Dear Lord, do not permit the flame of the seal to scorch the bond of love that binds us both! Bishop Conrad Martin, what have you imposed upon me with the dignity of the commission and with the burden of strictest silence!" As though a nerve from the document, resting on the thumping heart, governed the lips, they closed like a fine streak of blood.

Behind heavily draped windows in the late evening hours of June 1, nine postulants received their holy religious habit from the hands of Mother Clara in the oratory. Apart from the Mistress and the sacristan, there were no other witnesses present. With a short, easily intelligible statement, Mother Clara had explained to the postulants that, in these extraordinary times, this extraordinary manner of investiture was the only possible way to receive them into the religious family.

The investiture remained a secret by the immediate departure of the novices to daughter-houses.

Several weeks later Mother Clara's bell summoned her to the parlor. Reverend Moderator Klein wished to speak with the Superior General. The moment seemed opportune. Perhaps they might now think of a secret investiture; it was certainly high time.

As he was thus speaking, Mother Clara's hands slipped unnoticed under her scapular and lay firmly pressed on her heart, while she quietly declared after a minute of oppressive silence: "Father Moderator, I have already invested the nine postulants on June 1."

Reverend Moderator Klein could not believe that he understood correctly. He inquired, and he received the same answer in the same quiet, but decisive, tone; there was no word of explanation.

The silence that now followed was not only oppressive—it was unfathomable. Then the momentary hush was broken —reproach upon reproach: how she, a woman, could assume priestly, even episcopal rights; that such had never yet happened in the history of the community; that only pride and arrogance drove her to such functions; that the nine young ladies now wore an unblessed garment as a "religious habit"; that indeed the Episcopal See was vacant and a complaint to the ecclesiastical court was not possible at the moment, yet how painfully agitated the exiled Bishop would be on hearing of such transgressions on the part of his daughter; that he, the Reverend Moderator, would immediately inform the Father Confessor of the Motherhouse, Dean Schunck, of what had happened.

Dazed and speechless, Mother Clara sat opposite the excited man. Her hands remained concealed under her scapular. Like a hot stream her blood surged through her veins. The seal glowed, but her twitching fingers concealed the glow, while the bloody lines of her lips became still thinner. To the stern question of the Reverend Klein as to what she could say to justify herself, she answered calmly, "I urgently needed Sisters and the extraordinary circumstances of the times compel me to extraordinary action."

With an abrupt good-bye Reverend Klein left the Mother-house. A few minutes later Mother knelt before the Taber-nacle with a feeling of boundless abandonment and desolation. She no longer prayed, as she did after her disagreement with Sister Ignatia, that the glow of the seal might not singe the bond of trust between her and the spiritual Father of the re-ligious family; she knew that this cordial bond was not only singed but gutted and torn into shreds—once and for all.

"Conrad Martin! Your secret! But I will not reveal it even unto death!"

That thou wouldst vouchsafe to govern and preserve thy holy Church . . .

That thou wouldst vouchsafe to preserve our Apostolic Prelate and all Orders of the Church in holy religion . . .

That thou wouldst vouchsafe to grant peace and unity to all Christian people, we beseech Thee hear us!

Week after week Reverend Schunck had come to the Motherhouse—a genuine friend of the Sisters, a conscientious guide as a confessor. There was no care, no suffering, no joy in which he had not taken a fatherly interest.

Astonished, the Sisters wondered why the otherwise so kind and friendly priest now was so taciturn and so reserved. Mother Clara did not have to ask about it. Too clearly, she noticed the ever increasing estrangement. When, after the last meeting with Reverend Klein, she repeatedly received from the experienced ordinary confessor the admonition to put aside all arrogance, never to desire publicity, to flee pride as the greatest evil, to consider seriously the limitations of a Supe-rior's authority, she knew why Reverend Schunck spoke in that manner. He had been thoroughly instructed that she re-mained "obstinate toward the Church," that she "assumed rights" which belonged to the Reverend Moderator, and that she governed the community "independently of him."

Did not the seal of confession justify her to reveal her secret at least here? She did not reveal it. Bishop Conrad Martin had demanded: "Absolute silence toward everyone!" Reverend Father Schunck naturally had to become more and more puzzled at his penitent.

In accordance with the directions of Bishop Conrad Martin, she continued to handle affairs pertaining to the direction of the community independently. This gave her commanding nature a still greater air of assurance and decisiveness, so that Reverend Klein was more and more strengthened in his conviction: she is proud, arrogant, and self-willed. Indeed, how could he have surmised that Mother Clara's way of acting was prescribed by the secret plenary power given her by the Bishop. Although the two had worked together harmoniously and faithfully for a decade in promoting the welfare of the community, they now lived at odds even though the care of the community was likewise a matter of concern to both.

Now the Foundress experienced personally what Bishop Conrad Martin had so often told her: "Interior mortifications are more important than exterior austerities." The accusations and humiliations which she knew were circulating in clerical circles made her a genuine disciple and lover of the cross.

When the Lent of 1878 approached, Mother Clara had nothing more important to say in her circular letter to her daughters than: "Practice interior mortification with me!" What she wrote was the product of her own experience and a result of her daily battle against pride and self-will:

There can be neither true nor lasting love without mortification.

My children, above all practice mortification of your own will!

Concerning the work of our perfection, there is little to be done if our will is in conformity with the will of God and if we follow in humility and meekness the opposed will of others, especially of those given us by God as our Superiors.

Accept with love everything that is commanded; indeed, do more—mortify your own will!

Show that you belong to those noble souls who, through the grace of being brides of Christ, are imbued with love for the cross and find their entire joy in obedience, in self-sacrifice, in patience, in contempt, and in complete detachment.

Accustom yourself never to seek support and consolation in mutual friendship. Be content with the situations that arise from cordial sisterly love and upright obedience.

Seek renewal of strength by visiting our Lord in the Tabernacle and resting in his presence.

Help one another in mutual love! Above all, guard your tongue! Disputes rarely contribute toward one's salvation. Therefore, strive for greater holiness by practicing silence. The sins of the tongue added special bitterness to the chalice of suffering drained by our Savior. They were so deplored by the Psalmist that he implored God: "Hide me under the shelter of thy wings, safe from the evildoers who wrong me" Ps. 16,9.

To be forgotten and to avoid every inordinate desire and every complaint is indeed the true interior mortification that paves the way to perfection.

My daughters, above all mortify your pride, your vanity, your sensitiveness—and humble yourselves! "The greater you are, so much the more should you humble yourself in all things; thus you will find grace," says the Wise Man.

The faithful believe that our conduct and contacts are genuinely holy. It is difficult to receive marks of esteem without our hearts being moved by them. We are in danger of losing our spiritual balance and of falling into the sin of pride, and indeed into the greatest—namely, spiritual pride. For this reason, and justly so, our holy Father St. Francis lived in great fear at all times lest he succumb to pride. Hence, he was accustomed to speak to God as follows: "Lord, if you grant me anything, I commit it back to you because I do not trust myself for I am a thief when it comes to your treasure." Let us fear likewise—and indeed with greater justification—since we, despite our greatest zeal, shall never attain to the humility of our holy Father, St. Francis. Rather we must give back everything to God from whom it has come.

How the Sisters in the daughter-houses must have marveled that this time the Lenten letter of admonition, written by Mother, pertained exclusively to combating self-glorification. They did not as yet surmise the fundamental reasons for these motherly words. The Sisters at the Motherhouse, however, knew more. What they heard, while visiting the sick in their homes and on their quests for alms, embarrassed them and filled them with confusion.

What were they to think of their Mother? Could there be some truth in these reports? In any case, they definitely felt that the people were no longer as benevolent to the Sisters nor as generous in giving alms for the orphans as formerly.

In autumn it again appeared as though every possibility for Reverend Klein to have the investiture was out of the question. Nineteen postulants were waiting for the holy habit, and the daughter-houses were calling for help. Mother Clara was not intimidated by her bitter experience, which the first use of her plenary power had brought her. Her conscience was clear in spite of the reproaches which the Reverend Klein and the confessor heaped upon her. Consequently, she proceeded as before.

She divided the waiting postulants into small groups. Five times before the end of the year, the otherwise solemnly performed investiture took place very simply in the dimly lit oratory and during the stillness of the night. On the following morning everything was again routine. Several of the postulants' places remained vacant in the chapel. Those who had formerly knelt there were, after a night's traveling, already at their destination. One or the other daughter-house awaited them.

For one of these investitures, Reverend Klein had promised to come, provided nothing intervened. However, there was a repetition of what happened the first time. The little group arrayed in festive garb had to wait in vain for hours. Then Mother Clara took things in hand as though self-understood and made use of her plenary power.

The reaction was to be expected—the Reverend Moderator, a man of great conscientiousness and blameless exactness, came face to face with the fact that a Superior of religious women, "unauthorized," consistently encroached upon his rights. Could he remain silent in such a situation? The entire local clergy condemned the "illegal" activity of the Mother General. However, the accused spoke no word toward her exoneration. Her persistent silence gave rise to an ever greater estrangement on the part of the Reverend Moderator.

The tension increased when Mother Clara sought counsel and accepted energetic help from laymen in the difficult problems of the administration of the community. The Bishop had once carefully admonished her not to bring the Reverend Moderator into conflict with the civic authority. For that reason alone, she did not want to approach him now for counsel concerning questions that were difficult to decide; besides, the constantly increasing discord also barred the way. Still, in this time of need, she could not do entirely without a man's counsel; she obtained it from her brother and from a legal adviser who was a friend of the community. The fact that both men were seen frequently entering and leaving the Mother-house became a new stumbling block for clergy and religious.

In order to preserve her beloved orphanage from being dissolved by the government, Mother Clara had entrusted these laymen with the nominal government of the institution already in 1877 because the law against religious had deprived the Sisters of every educational activity.

All these independent measures, taken without the Reverend Moderator's knowledge, together with the exercise of "unjustified" ecclesiastical functions, confirmed him in the decision—Mother Clara Pfaender may no longer be Superior General of the community.

He made his arrangements quietly.

14

"If the seed does not die, it brings forth no fruit"
John 12:24

THE GREAT "PASSIONTIDE" WAS USHERED IN MORE SEVERELY than Mother Clara could have surmised. In alarming magnitude, the cross rose before her, and its weight became more and more oppressive. It was fashioned out of the divine will and with divine permission, out of her own weakness, and— may charity thus define it—surely an unconscious fault.

The first blows of fate struck her from without.

On July 16, 1879, Bishop Conrad Martin died in exile. For three years, the Sisters of Christian Charity of Mount St. Guibert in Belgium had concealed him as their local chaplain. Mother Pauline von Mallinckrodt succeeded in having the body of the esteemed Bishop brought in all secrecy to Paderborn, where he was buried on July 24 in the large cathedral with the approval of the government.

Among the numerous people who prayed before the grave of the Confessor Bishop, there knelt for many days—often for hours each day—a woman religious. Her tightly clasped hands rested upon her heart, and her lips appeared pressed mutely together rather than opened in prayer. However, that indeed was also a prayer.

The mute, prayerful woman was Mother Clara Pfaender.

With the death of the Bishop her extraordinary plenary powers, which he had imparted to her, had expired. To her, however, it appeared, as self-understood, that the secret commission reached out beyond the premature death of the Bishop and that he had placed upon her shoulders also the duty of silence not merely for the time while he was living. The Kulturkampf was not yet over and, in her opinion, the Bishop had imparted, to the community, secret rights and duties for the duration of the persecution of the Church. She intended to act in accordance with this opinion. She considered it the voice of her conscience, and she intended to follow it—even though it would cost her her good reputation.

The wound of her heart, which the death of her only trusted adviser laid open, was still fresh when a new blow struck this woman tested by suffering. In the spring of 1880, the government closed the doors of her orphanage. She was to give up the children, whom she loved—these children to whom the orphanage had become a real home.

Of what use were her objections? All remonstrances availed nothing in the face of the governmental decree. Benefactors who would adopt an orphan for God's sake were sought by newspaper announcements. Only a few responded. The majority of the children had to be sent back to guardians, to relatives, to Catholic or municipal agencies which were obliged to support them. Heart-rending was the departure of the little ones from the home they had come to love, and from the Sisters, who had taken care of them so faithfully. A few days later several of them were standing again at the convent door; the agencies or relatives had no place for them. Once more, Mother Clara took pity on these poorest of the poor and assured them of a lasting home in one of her houses.

The orphanage had substituted as a parental home for 313 children in Salzkotten from 1864 to 1880. Now the laughter and song no longer rang through the large rooms, and Mother

Clara's look passed sadly over the empty places in the schoolroom and in the dining room. In the dormitories, the Sisters devoted themselves with sad hearts to the work of taking the many children's beds apart and carrying them down to the basement.

Every evening, however, Mother Clara sent her blessing with holy water in all four directions to the children of her love and care.

How right the Bishop, experienced in suffering, had been when he set the worth of interior mortification and self-denial above the exterior austerities which she had once sought. There was no longer need of discipline to preserve in her the spirit of penance. This chastisement from the hand of God was harder, for she had to surrender the very essence of her life bit by bit. Her own work, however, still remained, and she was allowed to guide it in her own motherly way. She still had the love and confidence of her daughters; even if, to many, the activity of their Mother was unintelligible.

She knew that visitors had made her Sisters restless, that the Sister nurses who took care of the sick in the homes went to Sister Ignatia more and more frequently and plied her with anxious questions: "Was it really true what people in the country and in the city were saying? Even the clergy made no secret of the fact, that something was wrong with Reverend Mother." The troubled Novice Mistress calmed the confused Sisters and tried again and again to get Mother Clara to talk the matter over with the Reverend Moderator. No matter how much Mother and Mistress continued to plan harmoniously on all other questions and tried to keep the same pace in the guidance of the Professed and the Novices, on this point they did not agree. Even Sister Ignatia, from whom Mother Clara kept nothing else secret, knew nothing about the document which she had received from the Bishop in prison.

Reverend Moderator Klein quietly observed the continued independent manner of action on the part of the Superior of the community. He could not, and would not, suffer any longer an encroachment on his rights. Therefore, in accordance with the instructions given him in his appointment as Moderator by the Bishop, he demanded, in the beginning of the year 1880, that she "henceforth desist from any independent function in the guidance of the community." In implicit conviction of the legality of her action, Mother Clara obstinately refused to follow the dictates of the Reverend Moderator. Since she was unable to approach any publicly-recognized Episcopal Authority in Paderborn for advice, she turned for support to the Papal Nuncio Roncetti in Munich, in February, 1880. For the first and only time she revealed the secret of her special plenary powers by handing over the original letter of the Bishop. The Nuncio received the oppressed Sister with fatherly kindness; yet he urgently advised her to come to an understanding with Reverend Klein and thereby bring about harmony.

The Nuncio's counsel called for the observance of the orders given. There remained for Mother Clara no other way. Only hesitatingly did she promise to follow it, but her heart soon found the old objection. In spirit, she constantly saw the hand of the Bishop with his ring of episcopal might and dignity — and in this hand the document with its secret plenary powers. Constantly, there rang in her ears the Bishop's words to her under oath: "Absolute silence toward every one!"

The more plainly this remembrance loomed up in her soul, the more evident it became that the designated path was not the answer. Did she not think that the hand of the Papal Nuncio could unbind the seal which the hand of the Bishop had imposed? No one could read her heart, and never will it be fathomed why Mother Clara remained silent and felt herself bound by Bishop Conrad Martin's word.

The Reverend Klein and Mother General had indeed met for some time to discuss their differences, but they had not reached unity and understanding. Mother Clara relinquished none of her rights; she simply did not believe that they were null and void. If she had acted otherwise, she would have considered herself guilty of betrayal to the deceased. With her hand clasped to her heart, she declared: "I have the right to act independently and shall do so in the future whenever I feel obliged to do it." With word of neither confirmation nor excuse, Reverend Klein rebuked her, called her proud and arrogant, and condemned her activity as opposed to the Church. The accused felt her cheeks burning with agitation; but had she been able to reveal the secret on her heart with a single syllable or to extinguish its flames, her lips would have remained sealed.

A wall of silence stood between the two persons. Each one believed himself to be in the right. Mother Clara did not deviate in the least from the beaten path; the Reverend Klein considered it his duty to close this path to her forever.

This tension was evident to all in the Motherhouse. The Sisters did not yet know what was shattering the two pillars of the community; however, a dark burden weighed upon them all.

The councillors of Reverend Mother pleaded tearfully that she give some explanation why she considered herself in the right. The more they urged her, so much the more did her silence become impregnable. During their hours of perpetual adoration the Sisters prayed hour after hour "for an important intention of the community" as requested by Sister Ignatia.

To this slowly growing apprehension, another worry was added. The secret investitures, which were contrary to governmental regulations, had put the religious family into serious straits. The names of the newly invested Sisters were submitted to no authority. How easily an investigation of the Mother-

house or a daughter-house could reveal that new members
were being accepted secretly contrary to the explicit statements
of the law against religious! Was not the existence of the
community in Prussia at stake?

As a result of this serious situation, Mother Clara had
decided, at the beginning of 1880, to submit the names of
those already accepted to the authorities in the following manner. She would request the approval of the ministry for the
acceptance of a larger number of members. Having received
such a permission, she could then register the names of those
already invested. She saw in this act only a question of form
and certainly did not know that in such action she was trans-
gressing an ecclesiastical law.

The permission was granted, and Mother Clara felt at ease.
Should there be an investigation, she no longer had anything
to fear.

Her procedure, however, became known in clerical circles
and was represented as being unecclesiastical. Certainly, there
were reports that other congregations had acted in a similar
manner; they did not in the least intend thereby to go against
the laws of the Church. The confusion of the times made it
difficult to maintain clear vision. With great sorrow, Reverend Klein saw the community under his jurisdiction opened
to the criticism of the public. Was not the sovereign bearing
of the Superior General to blame after all?

He became more and more determined in his resolve to
have her quickly deposed.

On June 1, 1880, an invitation of the Reverend Moderator
called all Superiors of the European establishments to Paderborn. They were accustomed to meet annually in the Motherhouse for retreats and important business. But what was the
meaning of this meeting in the episcopal city? Without know-
ing the reason why but having some secret premonition, they

obeyed the invitation. Reverend Klein awaited them with a seriousness that perplexed them. He who was ordinarily quite skilled in words found it difficult to speak.

He was speaking to them as a representative of Episcopal Authority, he declared to those assembled. Then he revealed to the astounded Superiors what had taken place between himself and Mother Clara. With regret and severity, he condemned the "unauthorized" actions of the Superior General. Furthermore, he described these actions as contrary to ecclesiastical law and her headstrong persistence therein, as an opposition to Ecclesiastical Authority.

What then followed was a blow to the shocked listeners:

Decide:
    For or against Mother General—
    For or against Ecclesiastical Authority!

You cannot and you may not consider Sister Clara Pfaender as your Superior before God! You must deny her obedience!

Go home to your branch-houses! Tell your Sisters what you have heard here, and then let each convent send a manifesto to the Superior General:

That you condemn her actions in the highest degree, because they are not in conformity with the laws of the Church;

That you are no longer able to recognize her as your Mother, because of these regrettable circumstances;

That you no longer consider yourselves bound to her person by the vow of obedience!

And let every Sister put her signature to this manifesto to emphasize thereby her fidelity to the Church.

This mandate was incomprehensible to the Superiors. They should forego their Mother to whom they clung with child-

like love? To most of them she had been a teacher and a
Mistress. In the difficult times of the early foundation when
war, famine, and persecution reigned, all had shared in
Mother's burden and experienced her love at all times.

That they wore this religious garb and that they were permitted to function in this place as Superior—to whom else did
they owe thanks than to Mother? And all the Sisters at home
and abroad—who else had united them as a family of "Daughters of the Sacred Hearts of Jesus and Mary," than Mother?
How can a child renounce its Mother—and such a Mother,
who is most concerned about the welfare of her child?

Terrible struggles raged in the hearts of the Sisters. Each
one felt the penetrating glance of Mother upon her. O, if only
gratitude and sympathy had won the day! However, their
natural feelings were suppressed. Behind the shadow-darkened
picture of their poor Reverend Mother, there rose, lofty and
commanding, another picture—that of Mother Church. They
all knew with painful clarity that there was but one decision:
for the latter; and against the former.

Mother Clara's work appeared as though taken off its
hinges. Who should keep the orphaned and confused Sisters
together? Who should see to it that the shaken foundation be
stabilized, that the scandal, about which the people were
talking, be removed?

Reverend Klein made the following proposal to the Superiors: "I myself will undertake the guidance of the community for one year, and Sister Ignatia will be my representative."

The unsuspecting Novice Mistress had to be summoned
from Salzkotten. With deep emotion, she received the com-
munication of the Reverend Moderator; and with horror, the
command that she take over Mother Clara's office. She had
been the most faithful collaborator of Reverend Mother Clara,
had been her counselor and her admonisher, and now she
should be her successor after Reverend Mother had been

demoted? That she could not do. She pleaded and implored: "Not I! I am too intimately united with her. We would both break as a result!"

Only the severe admonition of the Moderator succeeded in changing Sister Ignatia's determination. In obedience to the Church, she accepted the commission in the presence of all the Superiors.

In the meantime, Mother Clara at Salzkotten had heard of the trips of the Superiors to Paderborn. Never yet had a meeting of the Sisters taken place without her knowledge or permission. This secret meeting could have only the vexatious conflict between her and the Reverend Moderator as a subject of discussion. Hence, she must take the matter in hand before it is too late. She suddenly decided to make a trip to Munich. The Papal Nuncio must help her.

With kindness the Prince of the Church listened to the oppressed religious, but he could give no other advice than that already given—namely, to come to an understanding and an agreement with the Reverend Klein, and thereby to submit to Ecclesiastical Authority.

Mother Clara returned home with a heavy heart. The hour of her arrival in Salzkotten was not known to the Sisters. For the first time, no one was at the depot to meet her. Exhausted by the long trip and crushed by worry, she arrived at the Motherhouse. She had scarcely opened the door to her workroom when the tinge of a sad smile swept over her countenance—a bundle of letters was lying on her desk. Surely, they came from the Superiors, from her faithful daughters. Now she would find it confirmed how they all suffered with their Mother and how they stood by her faithfully, in spite of all complaints.

She turned the latch on the door—in this hour no one dared to disturb her. The letter opener trembled in her hand as she opened the first letter. Then suddenly her face blanched. The letter slipped from her hand. With hands pressed to her heart, she sank back unnerved into her chair. She had read her death sentence—she no longer lived for her daughters.

Almost mechanically she took the second, and the third letter, and all the others. They were all alike: "We regret . . . ; we condemn . . . ; we fulfill a painful duty out of fidelity to the Church . . ." And then followed the names; scarcely one was missing. Mother's eyes glanced over the long rows of names, faltered here and there, and asked: "You too?—and you?" Even those whom she had considered the most faithful were no exception—they had all disowned her.

There had been several knocks at the door, first gently, then insistently, and finally, Sister Ignatia's voice was heard imploringly: "Please, do open the door!"

Mother Clara did not move. For hours she sat, as though benumbed, before the disarrayed batch of letters; her clutched hands lay folded upon her heart.

When the house had long been enveloped by the stillness of the night, she groped her way to the chapel. She sank down at her place in mute resignation. Before the altar, as always, there knelt two Sisters, and the quiet was broken by their muffled prayer: "In an important matter of the community, Lord have mercy on us!"

On the following morning, Mother Clara's pew remained empty. The Sisters found her in her cell; she could not leave her bed. Her already weakened heart had not been able to withstand the blow of the preceding night. She was given anxious care; however, it was a pensive service of love which the Sisters gave her. Each feared lest, by an indiscreet word, she touch upon the terrible episode that had taken place.

On June 14, an unexpected visitor was announced to the sick Mother. The Reverend Klein wanted to speak with

Mother Clara. What he had to tell her was said in one sentence, but what a radical change it meant for her life!

"You are released from the government of the community, freed from every responsibility, and may go to Bad Schwalbach temporarily to recuperate."

Without contradiction, with a mute bow of the head, Mother Clara received the decision of Ecclesiastical Authority. Did it still make sense to endeavor to come to an understanding as suggested by the Nuncio? Would she not meet with new reproaches and with the suspicion that ambition alone had now opened her mouth? Her heart was tired of struggling. She had only partly recovered, when she quietly made preparations for leaving. No one knew when that would be. Thus, the last night came, but the hard bed in the Superior's cell remained undisturbed. However, in the dark chapel, a broken heart struggled for the most difficult *Fiat* of its entire life.

In early dawn, the exiled Mother stood at the portal of the cloister to take her departure, which was to last forever. Sister Germana Bals, who had at all times been so faithfully concerned about the corporal welfare of Mother Clara, sobbingly accompanied her across the threshold; deep as an abyss was the sorrow of both. Yet calm trust was expressed in the last words of the departing Mother: "I must perish, but my work will continue. Since last night I have known this. May God protect you!"

Then she walked down the stairs. A postulant carried her light valise; no one else accompanied her—she wanted it thus.

Just once more her sorrowing glance took in the house that she had converted into a Motherhouse, which was home for her many daughters but which no longer sheltered the Mother; the house which she had transformed into a Tabernacle for the Most High, before which her children would continue to pray in the future.

Now she had given away everything to which her heart clung. Death had deprived her of her highly esteemed Episcopal Counselor and Guide. Laws inimical to the Church had closed her convents and schools and had deprived her of her work with youth. Fateful circumstances robbed her of the friendship and trust of beloved ones and made her homeless and honorless. The commission which was to give continuity to her work had become her own downfall.

At Bad Schwalbach, the ostracized Sister quietly went about her way. She sought consolation from no one; she bore her sorrow in mute resignation. Modestly and without reproach, she refused all solicitous care and consideration. Prayer calmed her and gave her strength, and even her sickly heart began to recuperate. When she was completely cured, she traveled to Metz. Her own sister was in charge as Superior of St. Blandina's Hospital. Here also she lived quietly and in retirement, devoted to the practices of piety.

In Bad Schwalbach, she had already learned that the Reverend Moderator Klein was visiting the houses of the community. It was easy to fathom the reason—he wanted to comfort the troubled Sisters and to strengthen them in God's providence. How easily they could have gone astray as a result of the incomprehensible events!

In Metz Mother Clara and the Reverend Klein one day stood face to face; not hostilely, but each with the consciousness of having acted correctly. She who had been deprived of her office declared that she intended to go to Rome in order to seek justice in the highest ecclesiastical courts. This resolve, the Reverend Klein could not oppose. He called the community together and in the presence of Mother Clara asked who wanted to be her companion to the Eternal City. No one stepped forth. A painful silence prevailed. The Reverend Klein repeated his question. Again he waited in vain. Then

Mother Clara looked from one Sister to another. No one could look at her. One after the other looked down, and no one stepped forth. Had not the Reverend Moderator let them be informed that Mother Clara's activities had been opposed to the Church? How then could she seek protection from Ecclesiastical Authority? Thus, with confused minds, they asked themselves.

The last in the circle was Sister Evangelista Hamboecker. Sympathetically, she observed the turn of events and, when it came to her turn, she stepped forward and said: "I will go along." A gratful look from Mother Clara rewarded her courage and fidelity.

It was in spring, 1881, that the two pilgrims arrived in Rome. They were able to find lodging in a convent, located near St. Peter's. This convent was remunerated by the Mother-house. In the shadow of the world-renowned cathedral, Mother Clara's hope for a prompt vindication grew.

How often was she to feel frustrated! The Ecclesiastical Authorities had for some time been made aware of the apparent unecclesiastical activity of the German religious woman. Therefore, again and again, she knocked in vain at the Curia. Because of well thought-out, but wrong reasons, she had not followed the path as directed for her at home by the Nuncio. That closed for her the approach to the court of last appeal in Rome—the Vatican remained closed to her.

She was called several times to the Secretariat of the Cardinal Vicar. However, instead of the hoped-for vindication, she was told, on February 11, 1882, either to lay aside the religious garb or to leave Rome. This hard measure was founded on her "disobedience toward Ecclesiastical Authority"—and the accused kept silence concerning the fact that it was exactly out of ecclesiastical obedience that she felt herself obliged to observe the command of her Bishop. Only with the Holy Father did she wish to speak. However, how could admission to the Holy Father be granted her, if there was doubt about her spirit of submission?

She prayed and hoped that, after all her waiting, the hour would yet strike in which she would be vindicated. The only thing that she attained in the Secretariat was the permission to remain in Rome, for the time being, in her religious garb.

She and her companion eventually found a modest refuge in the little house of a German woman, where they could lead a religious life in Franciscan simplicity. Prayer and penance filled the day.

Every morning the lonely Mother made her pilgrimage to the tombs of the Apostles; and, after spending some time there she made her way from one church to another. The stately figure of the prayerful woman formed so much a part of the pilgrim scene before St. Peter's that one can scarcely imagine the picture without her. But the longer she came, the more her steps lagged. Bent over, she climbed the steps leading up to St. Peter's. The golden cross on the cupola cast her a sorrowing glance.

The guards of St. Peter's looked in vain one day for the pilgrim. She remained away. Sick and wretched, she lay in her little refuge, lovingly nursed by her companion. The little flame of hope, that she might be admitted at least once to the Holy Father, Pope Leo XIII, was close to extinction. No one had to tell her that the goal of her pilgrimage would no longer be the throne of Peter. She felt with certainty that the time of her earthly pilgrimage would soon end. In the agonizing hours of the day and in the endless hours of the night, she saw her poor heart before the judgment seat of God, surrounded by a burning seal: he, whose right hand held the book with the seven seals, whose eyes were as flames of fire, alone recognized the secret with which she herself was sealed.

"Lord, how will it be sealed—to blessedness or to perdition? Be thou my vindication, when I appear before you in judgment! Be thou my vindication also on the last of all days when I, as Mother of many daughters, bear the crown of the harvest in your realm!"

The heart of the sufferer had detached itself from temporalities. Death will be easy for that person who daily practices dying to himself. The faithful nurse regretted that her patient could so seldom receive the consolation and strength of Holy Communion. She succeeded in getting a little place for her slowly dying patient in the German Hospice, at Compo Santo. There she could receive the best of care for body and soul.

With genuine pastoral charity, two priests offered to help the poor Mother. Dr. DeWaal, the very revered Rector of the hospital, removed her last temporal cares. She placed her testament into his hands on September 9, 1882. It clarified many questions concerning the property of the community.

The hospital chaplain of Campo Santo, a priest of the Society of Jesus, gave her the last rites. Reconciled to all the bitterness of her life, she saw with consolation her hour of death approach. No care and no visit disturbed her prayer. She remained deeply recollected; her emaciated and motionless hands were folded upon her heart. Thus until death, she guarded the secret of the burning seal, the flame of which gradually became extinct.

On October 4, on the feast of St. Francis, death sent its forerunner. It looked as though the Seraphic Father would greet his daughter on the threshold of eternity on his feast day —a daughter tired and purified in the fire of suffering. The dying Sister constantly implored him for help by weak ejaculations.

The death struggle continued.

Night came, but brought no release. The hour of death did not strike until the following day. Priests and Sisters held vigil at the death bed and were witnesses of the final word of one going home peacefully: "Come St. Francis, I am ready!"

Then the mouth, accustomed to silence, closed forever. As though drawn inwardly, the taut, pale lips were a touching symbol of the most difficult sacrifice that had been imposed upon her during life.

15

In the cemetery of St. Lorenzo

CORPORAL DEATH WAS LIKE A MILD "AMEN" TO THE LAW OF death for her, who had died spiritually a thousand times in the trust and in the opinion of men. Now the earth could open to take the motherly grain of seed into its bosom until a happy resurrection.

For two days the coffin, with its waxen corpse, stood in the choir of the Church of SS. Vincent and Anastasia. That was not unusual. Thus did the people who died in Rome customarily take their departure from this earth. Unusual only, was the picture of the deceased Sister in the habit of St. Francis.

Why was she not prepared for burial in her own convent? Was she a foreigner? Did she die enroute? Perhaps on a pilgrimage? Thus the visitors who came to pray tried to solve the mystery of the unknown religious.

Her hands lay folded high on her breast. They covered the pictures of the two Sacred Hearts on the black scapular—the one with the cross and the other with the piercing sword.

The sight of that corpse was a more eloquent sermon than if the mouth of the deceased had once again spoken: "In the cross of the Lord and in the suffering of his holy Mother, I seek my salvation; I leave it to the discretion of the merciful

119

love of both Sacred Hearts to manifest the secret on my heart. Now its flame is extinguished—as the light of my life. May God bless and comfort you when you see the revealed secret!"

The coffin was closed on October 7. After the funeral Mass a small group of German people formed the funeral procession to the grave. In the lead was Sister Evangelista, the faithful companion of her exile in Rome and the tireless nurse during her fatal illness. Tearless and with burning eyes she looked at the coffin; bitterness lined her numbed features.

The funeral procession made its way to the cemetery of San Lorenzo. In the register, the place of the grave was recorded as Section 30, Row 15, Grave 18.

After the last *Requiescat in pace*, Sister Evangelista stepped to the open grave and cast three handfuls of earth on the coffin in prayerful remembrance. Then she paused in prayer; and while her face tensed to hold back her tears, she let three more handfuls of earth follow in petition and apology in the name of all whom she saw in spirit gathered round this prematurely dug grave.

16

The secret revealed

NEWS OF THE DEATH OF THE FOUNDRESS DID NOT REACH the German Motherhouse until a narrow mound of earth covered Mother Clara's grave. The Rector of Campo Santo informed the community how pious and resigned she was in death. The news released mixed feelings: sincere sympathy that the humble Sister had to die in exile after waiting long and vainly for vindication, and relief that there would no longer be any fear of general confusion.

The Sisters did not have to be reminded to pray for their deceased Mother. They heartily fulfilled this duty. Mother Ignatia, who in the meantime had been chosen Superior General by the vote of the Chapter, carefully admonished the Sisters concerning the reputation of the deceased. In genuine loyalty to her, they were to mention the name of the Mother Foundress only with love and not in judgment, since the justification of man depends upon God. The first duty of her daughters was to bring the seed to growth and maturity by great love for their vocation: that seed which had sprouted from the one seed which God had placed into Mother's heart in a threefold basic commission:

Perpetual Adoration,
Education and formation of youth,
Nursing and care of the sick.

The seed and fruit were blessed, indeed, in the mission fields at home and abroad. Reverend Klein cooperated harmoniously with Mother Ignatia in governing the flourishing community. Exultant service of God, zealous striving for perfection, and manifold services of charity soon dispelled the last shadows which saddened the religious family. Mother Clara's name lived in all hearts but was seldom spoken. A holy silence enveloped the impenetrable occurrences.

Who would want to judge? Eyes cannot see beyond the surface.

For three decades, a dark cloud hung over the circumstances of Mother Clara's life. The severe disapproval, in which Reverend Moderator Klein persisted because he saw in the defamed Sister a stubborn disobedient religious, had subdued the desire of her daughters to visit the forsaken grave at Campo Santo. However, the muted, painful love for their energetic Foundress and above all for the warm-hearted Mother glowed more deeply in the souls of those daughters who had known her. Tear-filled eyes still glowed after many years when these Sisters spoke of her. Thus, the bond endured which attracted the love of all her daughters present and future.

And then happened what no longer anyone dared to hope—the portrait of the one overcast by a shadow brightened.

Sister Evangelista Hamboecker, Mother's companion in exile, had not returned to Salzkotten after Mother's death, because she had become embittered by the sorrow she had to witness. In a diary, she described the sorrowful experiences in Rome. In strong language, she accused the Sisters of infidelity and ingratitude. When she finally became aware of the motivation of Mother Clara's actions, she placed the entire blame of the tragedy on the community.

It was only after many years that this diary of the happenings in Rome came into the hands of the major Superiors of the community. These unjust accusations were not held against the confused Sister Evangelista; on the contrary, she was thanked in spirit for the faithful service rendered to the defamed Foundress.

All were sincerely grateful to her for the light produced by her diary. In obedience to the command of the Bishop, Mother had kept silence toward him who would have to condemn her for disobedience because he did not know the reason.

The knowledge of this tragic link revived the anguish of her daughters; but the joy of seeing their Mother vindicated surpassed the sorrow. When the Very Reverend Dean Schunck of Salzkotten learned and saw the proof of the existence of the episcopal, secret, plenary powers given to Mother Clara, he cried out in horror: "Then we have all done Mother Clara an unjustice; she has acted without sin."

All this happened in the year 1912, on the feast of the Exaltation of the Holy Cross.

"Why, O Lord, did you permit all this bitterness?" was the painful cry of many hearts. "For her sanctification and for our instruction," the remorseful daughters had to answer.

Reverend Schunck had often knelt in wordless prayer by the confessional in the convent chapel. He had been faithful confessor at the Motherhouse for decades. At no time had it been more difficult than during the unhappy disunion which had taken place during the Kulturkampf. Who could possibly have surmised what power dictated Mother Clara's way of acting! Even in the realm of the silence of the confessional, the secret found no entry. To such a degree she felt herself bound in obedience to the episcopal command: "Absolute silence toward everyone!" If she guarded the seal of silence so carefully and felt so obliged to keep it that she did not reveal it even once in the "Sacrament of the seal of confession," who would then be surprised that she shielded it from friends and enemies! She chose rather to lose the friendship and trust of men than to become disloyal in her promise to keep silence. Even though the seal by the heat of its flame might melt away her honor and her good reputation, her lips could not be opened.

She was accused of infidelity toward the Church, and her heart commanded: "Out of fidelity to the Church, be silent! You have promised it!"

All attempts to release the secret finally found no other answer than the tightening of the lips—an act dictated by her conscience.

Her soul grew in silence, but her heart broke under the stress of invincible pain.

Only ten years after her lonely burial in the cemetery of San Lorenzo, the cemetery in which the Foundress of the community was buried was leveled according to Roman custom. Her remains with that of the others were placed in one collective urn.

Thus even the conveyance of her body to Salzkotten for burial was denied her. However, her memory is kept alive in the cemetery of the Motherhouse by a marble tablet in the little chapel containing a picture of the Pieta, so similar to her own life's picture.

Wherever Mother Clara's daughters now abide: in Germany or France, in America or Holland with its missions in Indonesia—everywhere they are sowing the good seed, originally planted through the holy vocation of Mother Clara.

God must give the increase:
>   In Perpetual Adoration,
>   In the Service of Youth,
>   In the Work of Charity toward Sick Humanity.

He is the Lord of the harvest.

REMEMBER IN PRAYER
THE FOUNDRESS OF OUR CONGREGATION
REVEREND MOTHER
CLARA PFAENDER
BORN ON DECEMBER 6, 1827
AT HALLENBURG.
THE LORD CALLED HER TO HIMSELF IN ROME
ON OCTOBER 5, 1882.
IN THE CEMETERY OF SAN LORENZO
REST HER REMAINS.

✠

THOSE WHO HAVE INSTRUCTED MANY
SHALL SHINE LIKE THE STARS OF HEAVEN.

✠

Mother, at the throne of him, who has the harvest field at his feet and who carries the seed in his heart, obtain for your daughters the grace that they remain faithful in the harvest field of the world, so that he may look with pleasure upon the fruit of their labors.

To gain his good pleasure predetermines all our activities and makes us look forward to that final day when, with a thousandfold voice, we will call your name, Mother, and with you step before the face of the Most High.

Appendix

> "They follow thc Lamb
> Wherever He goes;
> And they sing a hymn
> Which no one can sing
> Except those who follow the Lamb."
>
> Apoc. 14:3,4

Mother, behold your faithful daughters!
Thousands, joyfully marching together
In the glorious procession of the virginal ones,
Bearing in uplifted hands your harvest —
The golden harvest of the hundredfold.
Mother, do you see the ears heavily ladened with grain?
A single kernel, falling from the Sower's hand,
Burrowed deep into the fresh-plowed earth;
From your soul, long grown accustomed to pain,
Your life's mission, Mother, gently budded forth.
Full many a storm your soul did weather —
This sprout of heart's blood did grow;
Truly, it was expedient that you die, Mother,
That we might live, as Franciscans, here below.
Has God rewarded you in return?
Yes, and that a hundredfold!

Behold! Mother, wheresoever you turn,
We bear aloft the ripe harvest—your reward untold.
When at length the measures of Life have run,
And Time has emptied into Eternity,
To you, it shall be granted to hear
How all your work is crowned by sanctity!
Hourly, we knelt before the Blessed Sacrament, at your behest,
As long as earth numbered us among her own;
Praying in adoration for the Church oppressed,
While nurturing the seed you've sown.
    Yes, Mother, at your behest —
    See now the ladened ears blest!
Although the Eternal City needs not the light
Of either sun or moon to reflect through,
Because the Majesty of God makes it effulgently bright;
Yet, Mother, behold the many that received the light of glory
                                      through you.
    Yes, Mother, at your behest —
    See now the Eternal light blest!
When every complaint at length is stilled,
And the tears of the sorrowing compassionately dried;
When pain and death no longer scepters wield;
Then, Mother, thank God your hand bravely tried
To soothe the pains that are so manifold,
By commissioning us to nurse the ill,
To support the crippled, to comfort the old —
See, Mother, how we've endeavored to do your will.
    Yes, Mother, at your behest!
    Now these laden ears are blest!
Into your firm, tender hands we place the harvest!
Carry it to the Barn where the Sower is enthroned.
As you approach Him with the Golden Treasure blest,
Your flock of children, the harvest canticle will intone:

"She went forth on her way and wept,
  Scattering her seed;
  But with joy we come,
  Carrying home the sheaves."